C

Acknowledgments

I would like to say a special thank you to David Courey, my buddy and still my Pastor, for his literary guidance, who met with me once a week for five years to help me write this book. David misses the Saturday afternoons we would spend together recounting the story, with lots of laughter and tears – and yes – occasional naps while typing!

It would be an understatement to add that this book would never have come to fruition without my sister, Sharon Moore-Bulmer for compiling all the facts from my journals throughout the years, and making it into a story.

Thank you to Jennie Murphy who edited this book, spending many hours of her spare time to help complete this project.

To the TTC Creative Group, Brian, Jim and Dave, thanks for jumping on board to create the book's terrific design, and becoming a part of this journey.

Last but not least, thank you goes to my wonderful wife, Monique for her patience and dedication in helping with some of the final details: you are the greatest blessing I have received after my long, hard journey.

I would like to let it be known that certain names of individuals and places in this book have been purposely changed in order to protect their privacy.

Billy Moore

Introduction

My name is Billy, and I'm an average guy. I just got back home from church on a Sunday afternoon, and I'm about to have some lunch with Monique. Then maybe I'll do some yard work around the little house I purchased a few years ago. Later I might watch some NASCAR on the Speed Channel, and if I get lucky the Islanders will win tonight. That's the New York Islanders (for those of you who don't know). Since 1975, they've been my favourite hockey team – come on, four Stanley Cups in a row – and I could care less about the Original Six!

My son, Tyler, is turning 35 this year. Man, time flies! We get together as often as we can, and when we do we have a good time with each other. My two older sisters and I enjoy our visits together, whether in Florida or on Manitoulin Island. Actually, I live a pretty run-of-the-mill, garden-variety-type life.

So why write about it? It seems like my life is like almost everybody else's. My body aches after a long day at the garage (I work at a garage and am a licensed mechanic). I pay my bills, but I wish I had a bit more cash for some of the finer things in life. What's so special about that?

Today I woke up feeling normal; no headaches, no shakes, no signs of illness. I can even remember what I did last night. It hasn't always been this way.

Today I will call my sister, Sharon. We'll chat about family stuff, talk about our plans for the summer, and decide that I'll come by for a weekend sometime in mid-July. It hasn't always been this way.

Today Monique and I will go for a walk and marvel at the fall colours. We just might get together with a few good friends and have some laughs together. Then as we retire for the night, we'll read the Bible together and pray; another great day will come to a close.

It hasn't always been this way.

Maybe I should start over. My name is Billy, and I'm an addict and an alcoholic. My life wasn't always so average. I had some wild times, which left me with a ton of pain and suffering and a truckload of destruction in my wake. In the process I lost a lot of stuff. I lost:
- my first wife,
- my son,
- my home,
- my parents' pride,
- my sisters' trust,
- my business,
- my trucks,
- my cars.

More than that I lost:
- my confidence,
- my self-respect,
- my hope,
- my values.

Most of all, I lost myself... I lost everything.

The story I want to tell isn't some rags-to-riches tale of how I pulled myself up by my bootstraps and made something of myself. Well, I might like to tell that story, but it isn't mine. It's not the story of one man's personal courage to fight against untold demons to become successful, rich and famous – I'd enjoy that story too! But my story isn't that glamorous.

The story of my life is how a good kid, from a good home goes so wrong… and how through a series of everyday events, stumbles onto the right fork in the road and rediscovers the path that God has chosen for him. It's the story of a desperate person groping in the shadows, and who, with one dramatic step, found himself in the light… walking into hope.

Chapter 1:
A Fine Church-Going, God-Fearin' Home... How Did This Happen to Me?

It was another Sudbury Saturday night. Only, this was Tuesday and it was a lot closer to morning. My buddy, Bobby and I had shut down the Nickel City Hotel – my hangout – and a bunch of us were crowding into Jerry's apartment to continue our party. Sudbury is still basically a mining town. It's a lot more than that today, but at its core – that's just what it is. One thing I still love about Sudbury is the people; just genuine, uncomplicated, warm people you can sit down and talk to. Sure some of them prefer to do it with a beer or joint in their hand, or over a few lines of coke like me and my buddies, but Northern people are just plain good folk.

I was born into a pretty regular, Northern home, really. My parents were good Christian people; church-going and God-fearing. My dad was a mechanic and ran his own garage. My mom stayed at home and took care of the house, just like on TV – kind of like Leave it to Beaver, except I had two older sisters and no brother. It was your typical, 1950's middle-class family. My sisters were 8 and 12 when I arrived. My parents were in their late thirties and were delighted to have a son. My dad loved sports and had played semi-pro hockey and baseball. I think he had similar plans for my life. My older sister Sharon will tell you the things she remembers of my early childhood.

When I was 4 years old, my Mother had her first heart attack. I don't remember much about when this happened, but I know she was never really well again. My sisters looked after me a lot. I guess I really had three mothers in a way, and subconsciously, became very dependent on female love and was really not aware of this until later on in life.

I went to Sunday school and church every week; I asked God to come into my heart when I was 5 or 6 years old. All of my family was very involved in the church and at first this was all I knew. As time went on and I got older, I was forced to attend church twice on Sundays and once on Friday nights. In those days, the Pentecostal religion was very strict. There were no dances, no movies, no playing cards and no sports or TV on Sunday, along with all the other Christian rules. As a young person, I attended youth group meetings and we went to camp meetings every summer on Manitoulin Island. This is where I discovered an interest in girls and started my life-long quest to get approval from women. Little did I know that later on in life, this problem of my co-dependency on women would rear its ugly head to me, time after time!

Ardith's Story

I was 8 years old when my baby brother Billy was born. Unfortunately, I came down with the chicken pox so I had to stay at my Aunt Trudy and Aunt Pearl's for a couple of weeks to prevent the new baby from getting sick.

Our Mom had so many medical problems before and after Billy was born and since I was like my Dad, an early riser, my job was to look after my little brother when our Dad went to work. I remember Billy coming to my door early in the morning and saying "Ardie, Ardie, op da door for your little brudder.

I don't remember a lot of my early years like they do, but my sisters were great to me and I have some wonderful memories from the days when I was young and they lived at home.

Sharon was 12 years older and I don't remember being very close to her when I was young, although I do remember lying with my arm under her pillow as she rocked herself to sleep. I recall Sharon playing the piano and her flute, practicing for recitals at church. She was always the mature, responsible one. Sharon had ambition and direction. She knew what she wanted out of life and went out and got it. When she was 18 she went away to teachers' college and almost overnight, it seemed, she went from being my bossy sister to being a real-life teacher. That was great, but unfortunately, in grades 4 and 5 she was my teacher. Some kids can do it: take the heat and pressure from family and friends to perform in school and be accepted – all while surviving their sister's rule – but I couldn't! I started to hate school!

You know how it is: your parents know every time you fail a test or mess up. Your sister is always holding it over your head with that look, and the kids in the class think you get special treatment or that you know what's on the test. But it was the complete opposite – it was awful!

Maybe that's when it all started. I'm the kind of person that when I'm not sure and the pressure is on, I make mistakes. I guess I began to feel very stupid. I would freeze when taking tests even when I knew the answers, because if I didn't do well, I knew I was in trouble at home. I still have problems this way today. It wasn't Sharon's fault, it was just the way I was wired. So looking back now, I see that this is when my shyness grew; being quiet and shy you will not seem as stupid.

Sharon and her husband, Ken, were very good to me. I guess there was a period of time up to and into my early teens, we did get closer. They took me out to the East coast with a stop at Expo 67. It was pretty cool. I remember long days in the car and I got really homesick once, but it was a good trip full of those picture-perfect moments.

Ken was a very good role model to me at the time. He worked for my Dad back then at the shop and helped me build a dune buggy before I even had my driver's license. Dad would haul it up to Manitoulin Island and I would drive it all over the place. Back then, there wasn't much traffic on the old, windy, dirt roads. I would also go drive it around the Sloss' farm yard right beside our camp. I found that having a cool vehicle got me attention and that, too, formed yet another pattern that became part of my life.

As time went on, Sharon and Ken had a daughter, Heather, and I remember spending a lot of time over there. Heather was the first grandchild/niece in the family so she was very special; everyone loved her, including me. I enjoyed playing with her, taking her for walks in her stroller and babysitting.

Ken decided he wanted more out of life than just working for his father-in-law in a garage and went to Teachers' College to become an Auto Tech teacher. A while later (I'm not sure how long after) he had completed his schooling he got a job teaching auto shop in Newmarket. So they moved away and began a new life away from all their friends and families. I missed Sharon, Ken and Heather – I suddenly became an only child as my other sister Ardith had already left home.

Ardith or Ardie, as we call her, was the black sheep of the family (before I took her place, that is). She had a hard time accepting all the church rules that we grew up with. She chafed under the parental yoke. One time, she was involved in an event that lead to having her picture in the local paper. This was scandalous because of the short skirt she wore, and as a result she was kicked out of the choir at church and given a stern talking-to. This episode – combined with some others – has understandably left a bad taste in her mouth about the Pentecostal church.

Being 8 years older than I was, we didn't play much together either. I remember one time, I was about 5 maybe, and I knocked at the front door of our house to get in because it was locked. She thought it was someone else, because I always went to the back door. There was a stool in the arch way leading into the living room, and she launched off of it in a hurry to get to the door. Well, she ended up hitting her head on the archway and split it open! I thought she was going to die the way she was bleeding. Needless to say, I got in big trouble for using the front door instead of the back.

Ardith was the playground supervisor in the summer time at Robinson Playground, right beside our new house. It was pretty cool having my good-looking older sister in charge of things over there. I'm not sure how old I was then but I was very proud of her and proud to tell everyone she was my sister.

Ardie bought me my very first Beatles album to my parents' dismay. In a Pentecostal home in the 60's, the Fab Four were definitely contraband! It made me feel cool because all the kids at school were listening to it at that time. My parents thought this was the 'devil's music' and didn't like it one bit. It was pretty clear from their attitude about the Beatles and the things I had heard at church that something had to give. So one morning I got up – took the album out of its cover and broke it into a million pieces. I felt like I had to do it, even though I didn't really want to. What I wanted was to be cool with the kids at school and cool with God, but the two didn't seem possible at the same time. Ardie took it very personally when I destroyed that album, even though I didn't mean to hurt her. And it left a scar...

The church tension for Ardith kept growing until she was in her late teens, which was when she left home and moved to Toronto. There she trained as a nurse, so I didn't see her much anymore. She came home to visit the odd weekend, and on one of these visits, she taught me about the birds and the bees (although, I pretty much had that figured out myself at the age of 13).

Now both my sisters were gone and my Mom was sick. It must have been tough on Dad to take care of me alone. Eventually, Mom got a bit better and my parents spent a lot of time at church functions, usually a few nights a week, so it felt like I was alone a lot.

Ardith ended up meeting Hugh (her first husband) around this time and they got married and moved to Waterloo. Hugh was a hobby race car driver and took me to some races, which was really cool, because I have been a car nut ever since I was 5 years old.

I had cars, cars and cars! Being alone a lot, I played with them constantly as a kid. This is when I activated a very vivid imagination. I could imagine they were racing cars in the Indy 500, although back then, I had to put my own numbers on them, because I didn't have many real race cars. Or I could pretend I was the owner of a large company called Zoom, with its fleet of vehicles, or just have a city with all the police cars, fire trucks and ambulances ready for action – there was always action in my city.

I also loved to play hockey, I was going to be the Team Canada goalie someday. My best games were in my base-ment with my cousin, Jim. He would be Foster Hewitt, giving the play-by-play action, and I was Johnny Bower, wearing Jimmy's pads. He wasn't much of a goaltender, but Jim grew up to be a preacher and has become very well known. Sometimes I would wear all his goalie equipment; I was in heaven and I must have won the Stanley Cup at least one hundred times. The love of hockey stuck with me growing up. I loved playing goalie but my dad didn't like this as he thought I would get my teeth knocked out. I played goalie every chance I could even though he didn't approve. Eventually he gave in and bought me some equipment and it paid off. Years later I made the Senior High School hockey team and played goalie on many teams for many years, winning boxes of trophies.

Playing with my toy soldiers was another favourite pastime. I had hundreds of toy soldiers and would have battles daily, the good guys always won. In reality in the 60's, we were smack-dab in the middle of the cold war, and most boys my age had heard stories about 'the big one...WWII' along with threats of nuclear extermination by the Commies. Our childish dreams of military glory hadn't yet been burst by the harsh reality of Vietnam.

Toy soldiers aside, I was scared to death of real war. I was quite young when the United States was involved in the Cuban missile crisis. My parents thought I was sleeping one night and they were talking about Sudbury (where we lived) as a possible target because of INCO being the biggest nickel producer in the world. I went out to the living room crying; I was so scared we were all going to die. We had food piled up in the cold cellar, and there were regular air raid drills. It was a very frightening time.

Another fear that all Christian kids grow up with, is something called the rapture. Pentecostals read the Bible pretty literally, so they take it seriously when it says that one day the trumpet will sound and the dead will be raised, and the Christians who remain alive on earth will be taken up into the heavens in a split second. The rest of humanity will be left behind to go through the dreadful judgment of the Great Tribulation.

When I was a kid we heard about the rapture at church almost every Sunday. It was sort of designed to comfort some and literally scare the hell out of others. I was one of the latter. I don't know how many times it happened, but if I walked into the house at a time of the day I expected everybody to be home and they weren't, I'd panic. I was sure the rapture had happened and I had been left behind. I would always try to call someone from the church like Ida Nelder or Mrs. Miesenhiemer, someone that I knew for sure was going to heaven. If they were home, I was safe.

Maybe it's called 'growing up Pentecostal', but my upbringing, for better or worse was centered around the church. My parents were devoted Christians, even if they weren't awfully fanatical. We saw Sister Wharton lead the Jericho March around the sanctuary and marvelled when Mr. Kjiersdam got blessed and danced in the Spirit with his eyes closed and tears on his cheeks. You could pretty much count on someone to give a message in tongues, while Pastor Cantelon knowingly nodded. It was kind of scary, often weird and sometimes wonderful – but to a kid growing up around the corner from the hockey rink in Robinson Playground, who was trying to muddle through grade 5 at Robinson Public School – it was mostly just too much!

So in school, after the years with my sister as my teacher in grades 4 or 5, I really became quiet and shy. I didn't like school anymore. I did okay in sports, but I was small and skinny with a brush cut and buck teeth. So I took my share of teasing, not any more than a lot of kids, but enough to cut deeply. I had failed grade 7 so I was left behind by my friends, and at that age, I just felt dumber and dumber.

By the time I got to grade 9, I had been in five different schools. We had only moved once in that time, but it was because we lived in a new subdivision that outgrew its school and the way that things worked out, our little class of a few would get all split up into two or three different classrooms at another school. It was either Group A, B, or C. I guess it went by your grades, the smartest to the dumbest and I was always in the C group with all the below-average kids; the tough kids and the bullies that smoked cigarettes, drank and even got high.

For a kid like me, it was all kind of bewildering; where things would end up and where I would fit in, I could never have guessed.

Chapter 2:
How It All Changed

When I was going into grade 10, there was a complication
at the school I went to. I wanted to switch from the 5-year
course to the 4-year course. Back then, that's the way the
curriculum was structured; you could choose between
the two courses to graduate. My marks were like 49.9% or
something, and I was going to fail. I thought that switching
courses might just change that, because the 4-year course was
a bit easier. Well my school didn't see it that way. My parents
didn't want me to fail again – as I had failed grade 7 already
– so my brother-in-law, Ken, looked into it, and at his school
it wasn't a problem. The next thing I knew, I was shipped
off to Newmarket (about four hours South of Sudbury) to go
to school for the next year! This was now the sixth different
school I had attended in my lifetime.

I remember the day I was sent to that school as being one of
the most difficult days of my life. I was at a school where I
didn't know a single person except my brother-in-law, Ken,
and he was my teacher! I really couldn't let on that I knew
him at first; knowing the teacher was definitely not cool in
1968, and it didn't seem like it would matter much anyway,
since it was the kids of the school that I needed to connect
with. It felt so weird, especially at lunch when I didn't know
who I could sit with and everybody was hanging out with
their gang, but there didn't seem to be a gang for shy and
nervous kids from Northern Ontario. For a long time, I felt
like a fish out of water. Some days at lunch I would just walk
around and not eat, or I would go outside and sit on the grass
in a secluded corner and eat my lunch alone.

Eventually, after some time I did make some friends at the church and at school. By now, Sharon and Ken had a son, Kent. So I spent a lot of time with their kids, and I got very close to them. It turned out to be a pretty good year of growth – some good and some bad, just like most teenagers, but I began to look up to the cool kids in my class that were into drugs and drinking.

I would go home to Sudbury every chance I got so I could see my friends. I would be so excited to be home that I wouldn't eat supper, I would just start calling everybody and go out. It was on one of these trips home that I first started experimenting with drugs (when I was with a church friend, who will remain nameless). We scored a little hash and went out to Kelly Lake Road to smoke up.

It didn't seem to do anything to me, but the fact that I did it was cool. I was being a rebel, going against the grain of all I had been taught in church. "You say you want a revolution, well, you know..." as The Beatles song puts it. It was no big deal and besides, it was just something I did that one time. It wouldn't change me or anything for that matter. I was a lot like all the others kids: I wanted to fit in, be cool and get the girls to like me. And let's face it, I was worried. I was plagued with fears, probably like everybody else fears like:

> I wasn't smart enough,
> I wasn't good-looking,
> I was too skinny,
> I wasn't good enough,
> I wasn't strong enough.

I was sure there was something wrong with me! I know now that this is normal teenage thinking – just part of growing up! But I was starting to be convinced... just maybe I WAS wired differently. It was an awkward time. It seemed like I had a hole in me deep inside; an uncomfortable, icky feeling. When I smoked up, that feeling would go away.

But instead of talking to someone I could trust or even going for counselling to learn how to deal with these feelings, OR asking God for help, I made a choice to keep on experimenting with drugs and alcohol. I was 17 the first time I took a drink and smoked a joint – late in life by today's standards! Nowadays, the age of first starting to experiment is 12 years old, and sometimes younger!

It was MY choice, and it did the trick! The drugs and alcohol made my fears and worries go away. I could be "cool" and escape those fears (or so I thought, not realizing how temporary and permanent at the same time the fix would be).

I made new friends – those who also did drugs and drank. I didn't need God anymore (or so I thought), and these were the best friends I ever had. I finally fit in. Marijuana (pot, weed, smoke – whatever you call it) had become my drug of choice.

By this time, I had moved back to Sudbury and started to attend my seventh school. This time, I knew a couple of guys that were going there. Brian was one of them, and I had known him from the old days in Robinson (which is a subdivision). He had gone to the Catholic school there and we had been Blood Brothers in a little club we had. These guys I knew liked to get high; it was the thing to do. I worked part-time at my Dad's garage, pumping gas and with his help (a lot of help), I bought a 1970 Dodge Super Bee (one of the original muscle cars). It was new, bright yellow with a black leather interior and a big engine with lots of horsepower. All

17

of a sudden, I began to get a lot of attention; it might have had something to do with pulling smokers with it in front of the school just about every day!

We would pile in, get high and go cruising, or hang out at A&W which was a very popular spot. I was also the backup goalie on the High School hockey team, and would start the odd game. A couple of girls Brian and I knew were cheerleaders, and they would chant my name and cheer me on. I used to get so nervous that I would feel sick! I let in a lot of goals, but gained much experience that year.

It was in this year that I had my first mind-blowing experience. All the time before, I thought I was high, but I wasn't really. This one night at a party at Brian's parents' house, it happened. After drinking and smoking dope all night, I began to feel like I never had before. I was very scared! I went outside and stood in the snow, trying to come down from being high. I didn't like it. Everyone was laughing at me, and I was trying to tell them that something was wrong. Finally after a few hours, I came down enough to feel like I was back to normal.

For awhile after that, I didn't smoke anything because it had scared me so much, but I had to if I wanted to hang with the crowd I was in. I also met my first girlfriend, Karen, around this time. Brian went out with her best friend. There was always a party somewhere, so we would go to someone's house and drink, smoke dope, and make out. Life was now good; I fit in and I was cool.

I sold my Dodge Super Bee and bought my first hippy van, complete with Canadian flags painted on the side windows and a bed in the back. I even had kept the chrome wheels off the Super Bee and put them on it. Once, during the time I was dating Karen, my Dad went looking for a wrench in the glove compartment of my van, and he got a big surprise: a bag of dope! He freaked out and proceeded to march me and Karen up to Pastor Cantelon's house, who happened to be my first cousin. He talked to us about it, and made us swear on the Bible that we would never touch dope again. Well, we did what they asked, but just so we could get out of there! My parents did what they thought was right to try and stop my path of destruction, but nothing they did or said could have changed my mind. This was the direction I wanted my life to go!

In the summer between grades 11 and 12, I met a guy who influenced me greatly. He was the cousin of a family friend. I first saw him at a wedding and he had on a tuxedo with a pair of old, white running shoes. I thought that was so cool. He was a real hippy: long hair, scruffy beard... groovy, man.

I started hanging around with him a bit over the next year or so. He was a few years older than me and he taught me the hippy stuff that I wanted to know – peace, love, and all that junk – anti-establishment rhetoric about rich fat-cats with empty lives, how material things weren't important, just getting high and grooving to music. There were very few of us in this circle, and we were quite cool.

I was still going to school, but left it all behind with only one semester to go in grade 12 so I could follow the hippy movement. I moved out of my parents' house, and lived in this dingy basement apartment for awhile with a bunch of other guys.

I always dreamed of being a professional hockey player. It's a dream I gave up on, though. That next year, I would have been first-string goalie – and I think I might have had a shot at the big leagues along the way. A lot of guys I played with got scholarships to Colleges and Universities all over the place, and others from the North made it to the NHL – but not me. No, I had a better plan: I quit school to become a hippy! Who knows what could have happened had I stayed in school. Later in life, I took hockey back up and I was a pretty good goalie, if I do say so myself. But I was too old and it was too late.

My hippy friend moved away and I really couldn't live that life 100% anyway, but I was still going to give it my best. I had the hair to do it, as well as a growing devotion to the mighty doobie. But I soon found out that being a hippy actually costs money! Since I needed cash, I went to work full-time for my Dad. He and his partner hired me and I did eventually get my mechanics' license. I had terrible work habits – often arriving late and leaving early, but my Dad always covered for me. He really was the best Dad anyone could ever have! I regret that I didn't realize it while he was alive.

Since I had moved back to Sudbury, I saw less and less of Sharon and her family. I did stay with them one more time for a term of Trade School when I was 24 years old, though. There was the odd visit, but as my addiction grew (and I didn't even think I was addicted then), it was hard to spend time with them. I felt uncomfortable. I thought they were 'Bible thump-ers' and I didn't want to be near them. Plus, I needed to sneak off every once in awhile to get high so I could feel somewhat normal around them.

Chapter 3:
Losing Control

I continued using drugs and sometimes alcohol more and more. I really liked it! It was fun! It took a little more each time to get the same effect, but it was worth it to feel so great, even for a short while. Pot became my drug of choice – drinking was only an occasional thing. I used pretty much everything around from time to time: mushrooms, angel dust, LSD, MDA, mescaline, and speed. Hash and weed was what I did all the time.

I was still going to church every Sunday, but only because I had to. I had better have had a good excuse if I missed it, because I had to face Dad every day at work. So I would drag my sorry and somewhat disoriented carcass out of bed each Sunday morning. My Sunday appearance was somewhat out of the ordinary for a Pentecostal church in the early 70's. Straggly hair and smelling like the night before with that sort of strung-out look on my face marked me as an outsider, even wearing the required jacket and tie! And that wasn't so bad, I thought; I wanted to look like an outsider.

One night, we were having a few puffs on the old dirt road, which was considered the edge of town. We were so involved in what we were doing, that we failed to notice a car sitting a couple of hundred yards away. All of the sudden, it came at us. The red lights started flashing as it skidded to a stop beside us. It was a police car. My friend threw the dope under the car (a nice chunk of hash). We made up some lame story about why we were there.

The one cop asked, "What did you throw under the car?"

"Nothing," we said.

"Okay, back up the car" he replied.

So we did. But it was winter and night time – and nothing was found – so they let us go. We went home and got my snowmobile, rode back to the spot, dug around a bit, and "WOOHOO!" – We found it, went back home and finished it off.

Another time, a friend (the same one I had my first toke with) and I were headed to Florida to meet our parents for Christmas. We were stopped at the border. The Customs Agents went through the van and found a marijuana seed. They then proceeded to rip the van apart and strip-searched the two of us, finding two ounces of pot in our underwear. All they did was take the drugs, gave us a large fine (which ate up a good chunk of our party budget) and said, "Get out of our country, and don't come back!"

Well, we kind of had to get to Florida, or we would have had to tell our parents what happened. We just couldn't do that, so we decided to go to another crossing. This was around 1970, so the technology wasn't what it is today. They did the regular routine check, then looked me in the eye and asked, "Have you ever been refused entry to the USA?"

I gave him my most earnest "No."

The Customs Agent looked at me – then at the computer screen – paused for a minute and said, "Okay, then."

And we were on our way. The only problem was, my old van died just as we pulled away from the booth. We were in a panic! We had to get it going before they found out about us. Luckily, it was only a loose connection on the battery. The van fired up, and we got out of there as fast as we could.

The next town we came across, we saw a long-hair walking down the road, so we stopped and asked him if he knew where we could score. He took us to some guy, we bought a nice bag, and off we went. We made it all the way to Florida and our parents never knew anything about our little escapade.

A few years later, I had my police record checked for Canada and USA, and there wasn't anything there! Strange! The Customs Officials must have just pocketed the dope and the money and not told anyone, either. That's the way it was in those days – just one big happy party for everybody!

By now I was getting high almost every day and was definitely looking for love – always in the wrong places, of course. I had a few girlfriends here and there, but no one that I wanted to spend the rest of my life with. Just as well, because it wasn't shaping up to be much of a life to spend with anybody.

I was a car nut back then. In fact, I am still a car nut and I always will be! I went from cars, to muscle cars to custom vans. Back in the 60's I had a couple of your typical hippy vans with the flower power decals and Canadian flags painted on the windows. My buddies and I would go for a trip every year down to the States, ending up wherever and partying with whoever. This was during the Vietnam War, and we got a lot of different reactions from different people. A lot of guys our age were in the army, so the girls loved us, but the older people didn't. I think they might have thought we were draft dodgers or something. One time we were walking down the street in downtown Rochester and people parted as we came, shoved up against storefronts and crossed the street, because we seemed like such freaks. And – to tell the truth – we kind of liked it!

On one of our adventures, Brian, Coop, and I were driving down the New York State Thruway. This was a year after "Woodstock" and we were driving right through that part of upstate New York. We picked up this hippy chick who was hitchhiking. She lived in New York City, she said, so that's where we decided to go. As she gave directions, next thing we knew we were driving on Broadway! We pulled up to this big Park Avenue condo. A man in uniform came out of the building and said, "Hello, Miss Emily." She replied, "Hi Jasper," and tells us to get out of the van. So this guy with tassels and epaulets gets into the old hippy van, and drives it away to park it. We had quite a laugh as we watched in disbelief. Then we proceeded to her parents' penthouse for a bite to eat and a look at the view. Later, she took us to Greenwich Village where we met some real New York City hippies and hung out for awhile. As we were there, Emily just disappeared into the crowd, and we continued on our journey to nowhere in particular.

It was around this time that I stopped going to church, or only went once in awhile to keep my mother off of my back. I was using drugs more and more. My buddy, Ernie and I started getting into customizing vans, because vans were the cool thing just then. Ernie and I have remained lifelong friends. We both have taken similar paths, looking for direction in one more toke or just another snort. To this day, Ernie is the most talented body man you could ever meet. The guy could mould metal like it was a piece of plasticine, and could bronze weld (a lost art today) like Leonardo da Vinci. So we made a great team – me the visionary dreamer – Ernie, the auto body artiste.

This is when I met Jean, my future wife. Jean was then – and still is – a very beautiful lady. I met her on a Wasaga Beach wild weekend. Everyone told me that she was out of my league, but that only made me try harder. She was everything I wanted: beautiful, with curves and mounds in just the right places and smart, too. After all, this girl actually had a real job! I saw fireworks when I was with her.

We dated for a year and then got married. We were too young. I think we got married just so we could live together and get out of our parents' houses, because shacking up was just not an option. We couldn't face the heat from either of our parents, so we just bit the bullet and did the "right thing". Only, it turned out in so many ways to be the wrong thing. We separated time after time in the 23 years we were together. We both had issues that we never dealt with, and disaster was an inevitable result.

I never felt truly loved by Jean. It always felt like she was still hung-up on the last guy in her life. Of course, I may not have been the most sensitive lover, either. So the wounded boy, feeling rejected and unwanted, found solace in other places. We would separate and I would go off and party, having affairs and telling myself it was okay under the circumstances. It was the coping mechanism that had led me to drugs in the first place, and now it was playing havoc with my marriage. It would haunt me for a long time before I recognized it for what it was. Eventually, after a couple of months of carousing and sometimes up to a year, we would get back together again and carry on like nothing had happened.

Eventually, Jean became pregnant with our son, Tyler. I had always wanted a little boy to play hockey with, to play catch, and to work on vans with. Things started off that way, and everything was good. He used to come to the shop with me when he was very young and peddle his little car all over, while I would work on the van. He would get so dirty, and Jean would spend hours getting him clean again. But when it came to sports, Tyler didn't particularly care for them, and I did. The tensions grew. I forced it on him, and he would balk. In the end, it seemed the more I wanted him to play sports, the less interested Tyler became.

Jean got a job at the Regional Police station, and that opened up a career she has continued to this day. My Dad had some connections that helped her, and she began to do shift work there. It was hard on me, because I could barely take care of myself, let alone a little boy. Tyler and I spent a lot of time together when he was young. I wasn't much of a cook, so we ate at McDonald's a lot of the time. Don't get me wrong... I love Tyler more than anything, but I wasn't a great father in a lot of ways. I would smoke up right in front of him all the time. I played with him a great deal and thought I was doing a good job, but I was constantly stoned.

I see now that when someone is stoned or drunk – no matter what they're doing – it's not really them doing it! Whatever else I said or did, for me getting high came first, and Tyler picked up on that right away. At school, teachers taught about the dangers of drugs and how dope was bad, and it affected how Tyler looked at me. He deserved a committed father who had time for him, not a doper Dad who was trying to fit him in between tokes. I was going through the motions, but I was somewhere else while I was doing it. Not a very good role model!

It didn't show up all at once. On the surface, we had a pretty good relationship until he was about 14. At least he didn't seem to mind being with me. But mostly we were doing my thing: working at the shop, out to ball games and hockey games (where Tyler became the unofficial baby-sitter of the other kids), and generally having a good time – at least, what I considered to be a good time.

But then my addictions grew worse. Altered states of consciousness had been a large part of my life until then, but at some point I crossed a line where my entire life became about getting high. It wasn't any longer something I did to get through the day; instead the day was occupied with finding ways to stay high. Tyler was getting older, and I was getting more distant. He could understand that this wasn't what a parental relationship should look like, and me, I wasn't aware that anything was out of the ordinary. It caused us to grow apart. It was never his fault at all! I just changed and my only priority was being stoned.

My best friend, Ernie and I continued to do some cool paint jobs and customizing on vans, but that wasn't enough. One day after a few joints, we came up with this great idea. What if we chopped 8 inches out of the roof of my full-size van? It would take a lot of time and money to do. Did we have the skills to get the job done? And what about the cash? Of course, a lot of the money went for the dope we needed to keep us going. So here we are, two pot heads about to take a fairly new van and cut it all up. My dad just shook his head and said we couldn't do it, we would never get it finished and it would be a pile of junk! None of our buddies thought we could do it, and it became kind of a joke. But we did. It took six months – working every night and weekends – but we actually did it. And the truth is, it was way cool!

At first we called it 2001: A Van Oddity. We had a lot of fun with that van and it became one of my obsessions at that time in my life. In fact, we eventually renamed it Obsession. We were still finishing the interior during the first car show that it was entered in. Adding some really cool candy apple flames was the finishing touch, and we began taking it to shows all over. It won boxes of trophies and prizes, but the best was having the van photographed for magazines that were published all over Canada and the USA! We kept adding more and more customizing to it and different paint jobs. We continued to have great success, both in magazines and shows. We were van heroes! It didn't increase my income or improve my marriage, but it did raise my popularity – particularly with the women. In fact, Jean grew intensely jealous over Obsession, and rightly so since I had a lot of parties in the back of the van (which had a bar, a TV and an eight-track, a bed, and psychedelic lights). "Yeah, baby, yeah," as Austin Powers would say.

Now in my mid twenties, I was getting high morning, noon and night, and having a hard time figuring which was which. I somehow managed to get to work every day at my Dad's auto shop, though I showed up late more often than not. Dear old Dad would always cover for me. There were times when Jean and I were apart, I would pull my van into the shop at four in the morning and sleep in it until Dad came in and woke me up for work. And like the Dad he was, though I'm sure his heart was breaking, he would bring me toast and coffee to get me started.

In the day I would work at the shop and at night I would work on my van, then go home or to the bars (depending on whether I was separated at the time or not). In the summer I played ball on a couple of teams, one with my childhood buddies, Brian, Coop, and Jimmy; in winter it was hockey, three or more nights a week. Of course, I would get high before every game and then drink beer after. All this would have to be choreographed with babysitters and grandparents for Tyler because Jean worked a lot of night shifts, and I played most of them. And when I did stay home – I wasn't much company for Tyler – recovering on the couch from the night before.

My sister Ardith and her first husband got divorced in 1980, but they had two children: Tracey, and Wade. As I got older, I found that she was much more liberal about things. We had been raised in the old-time Pentecostal way, but it seemed like both of us had rebelled a bit – so I would visit her and her kids more than my other sister, Sharon, who was still a devoted follower. I remember telling Ardie I could quit anytime, but I didn't want to. I was just lying to myself and she knew it. But still, Ardie was very good to me and even helped me financially at times.

My parents did everything they knew how, but not knowing of my addictions – nothing helped. I had all they could give: a new car, a job, the down payment on my house, bills paid if need be – whatever I said that I needed. Every Sunday, my Dad picked up my son for Sunday school. At one point, I had even promised my Dad that I would never drink! He had made the same promise to his Mother in 1933 and had kept his word. I made it and then did exactly as I pleased! How I regret that! A promise to the people that loved me the most meant nothing to me. But if you were a buddy, it was a whole different deal. I always kept my promises to them and actually thought I was a very trustworthy person.

But broken promises lead to increasing guilt, and while I could lie straight-faced and stare them down, there were other times when I couldn't bear to look my parents in the eyes. When my Mom would plead with me to come to church on really special occasions and then go to some family function, I would stare at the ground with shame and remorse and say, "Okay."

In 1982, my mother died. I was 30 years old and finally free from the guilt trip of looking into those eyes. Things went from bad to worse.

Chapter 4:
Mom – Remembering Elaine Moore

My mom had heart problems ever since I was born. I remember that she couldn't do any physical activities at all. She would get chest pains just walking up a flight of stairs. My parents ended up spending time in Florida every winter because she couldn't stand the cold air of a Northern Ontario winter. I would get out of school to go with them to Florida most of the time. Mom would try to get me to do my school work every morning, but I was never too happy about it.

We would spend – it seemed – all summer at Manitoulin Island. My dad would leave some old wreck of a car with us to get around and he would come up on weekends. Mom didn't drive much, so my Aunt Russ did all the driving. Every summer for two weeks, my family observed a Pentecostal tradition: Camp Meeting. To the uninitiated this might sound like fun: paddling canoes on the lake, waterskiing, fishing, and maybe a panty raid at the girl's camp – but it was none of those things. It was one thing: church. Morning, noon, and night... church. As a kid, all I wanted to do was play or go out in the boat or really do anything, but NOT CHURCH! I have to admit, I slept through a lot of those services and so did a ton of other kids.

We would pile in the old car and drive up to the church camp on the dusty, windy roads. The cars we had were old (like I said) and had holes in the floor. We would eat dust every time we drove in them. I still remember that taste – gross!

The evening services were the craziest. The horns were playing away in that makeshift orchestra something like "Victory in Jesus" or "Power in the Blood"; mosquitoes the size of spitfires had a captive audience to feed on, and old J.H. Blair would be raising the offering with that raspy voice of his. I can still remember the smell of that place with the sawdust floors and the wooden benches – much the way it is today, except the floor is cement now. The sweaty evangelist would preach in the thick, July humidity and I would curl up in the safety of my Mom's lap and drift away.

One summer morning at Bible study when I was about 6 or 7, I did give my heart to Jesus. The altar call was given (which happened twice a day) and on that one morning, I just found myself drawn up to the front. I repeated the sinner's prayer, confessing all my seven-year-old sins and I was 'saved'. I made my Mom proud, became the story of the week around our camp, and gave her some great news to tell Dad when he came up on the weekend.

It should have ended there. I should have grown up to 'serve God' and 'stay away from sin'. All those old camp meeting clichés should have been true in my life! But they weren't. How could my parents imagine the painful journey that would eventually bring me "Safe in the Arms of Jesus", as the old hymn put it?

Mom was so good to me, not unlike any other mother, I suppose. But in my family, I was the youngest and I was spoiled rotten. If my Dad said 'no' to something I wanted, Mom would always come through for me. Once a month (or something like that), we would go to Eaton's downtown and I could pick out a new Dinky toy. They were the best: bigger than the Hot Wheels of today, and much stronger too. My son

Tyler, still has a few of them from my childhood, although they are all scratched up.

I very much took my Mom for granted. She was sick, yes – but she always pulled through; a while in the hospital and then she would be back home. And while her heart was weak, it was tender for the less fortunate. She went out of her way to help a lot of families.

We had cousins who lived about an hour away, where Mom was raised in Massey, Ontario. They liked to drink and party. They had four little kids, and Mom would always make sure they had what they needed. I used to hate going there because their lifestyle was unlike anything I had ever seen before. I was very sheltered from all of that. My parents never drank at all or even smoked, and I just assumed everybody was like that! But every time we visited, Mom would bring groceries, and at Christmas, gifts for the kids. I sometimes thought others took advantage of my parents and I didn't like that. But that was the way my Mom was: she loved to help out, mostly for the kids.

There were many in the church too, that she made a point of helping out. Her memory lives on with those who knew her. When she died, I was a very active pot head. Nothing got to me. Why worry, just smoke another joint – it will go away! So that's what I did, and it worked... until years later when I cleaned out my system. Then, the memories came flooding back.

I remembered the day she died. I got to the hospital and was told to go see her. She was already dead. They said to talk to her; they said that she could hear me. She wasn't in a private area at all. There were other people on stretchers with various injuries all around her. I just remember her lying there with her mouth open, no teeth, pale and DEAD! It was not the way I wanted to remember my Mother! That's why when they tried to get me to see my Dad when he died, I refused. I don't think anyone should do it; it's not a good memory!

After that, we left the hospital. I talked to my Dad and told him I was going to take Tyler to his hockey game. Imagine that! I left my Dad alone! My sisters hadn't arrived from out of town yet, and I just left him. What was I thinking? Thank God Andy was with him. Andy was a boarder who had lived with them for awhile – and at least he was there for Dad, even if I wasn't. I turned to the best friend I had: weed. I smoked a joint, maybe downed a few beers. I can't remember altogether what I did, except for this: I wasn't where I should have been.

Doesn't that tell you something about addictions? How screwed up a mind can get when you forget who really matters; you numb your soul instead of allowing it to feel the pain of sorrow, called love. It was easier for me to run from the situation than to deal with it. No matter how hurt my Dad was, I only thought of me!

Like every recovering addict, I wish I could make up for so many things. With my Mom and Dad, I wish I could say the things they needed to hear, and do the things I needed to do to show them I loved them. I wish, sometimes, I could go back to those hot summer evenings at Manitoulin Island and curl up in the safety of my Mom's lap and start all over again, but I can't. It's over; it's too late and I regret it.

Chapter 5:
Dad – Remembering Tommy Moore

My Dad was a Northern guy: born in the North, lived in the North, and died in the North. Every winter, he would spend multiple hours building a rink for me in our backyard. Around Christmas, he'd put the boards up, then he'd pack the snow down for awhile; and then night after night, he'd come home from work and water it before dinner and then again later, before he went to bed. There wasn't any playground in the area at that time, so a lot of the neighbourhood kids would congregate at my place for shinny.

Eventually, they built a full-sized hockey rink at the playground over at Robinson School, right next door to our house. It didn't have any lights though, so Dad would run a long extension cord over with a couple of big spot lights hanging on it. I could dress up at home; walk over with my blades in the snow and skate and play to my heart's delight, in the cold, crisp night air.

Dad worked very hard at his Auto Repair shop, but I would always get him to come downstairs to the basement to take some shots on me at night. I loved playing goalie, and the basement was the only place he would let me do it, because he thought I would get my teeth knocked out if I played that position. So he would shoot a tennis ball at me until he was tired, but it was never enough for me.

When I got into organized hockey, he coached our team for a couple of years. I had to play left wing, because – you know – the TEETH! Eventually, I started to play goal on the high school team. He never came to any of my games though, but I genuinely think it was because he thought he would jinx me. Later on in my hockey life, when he did come to watch me play, I had a horrible night and let in 10 goals. After that, it was a long time before he ever came again. He thought it was his fault, but I just had a really bad night!

My Father was an avid hunter. We would get up in the early morning, hours before the sun rose, and drive forever. 'Moose Crik' (Northern guys never say 'creek') was his favourite place for ducks and partridge. I have a print hanging in my rec room, which reminds me of the early mornings there, as the fog was lifting to reveal the sunlight.

Dad loved to take me hunting with him. He was so proud of me when I shot my first partridge. He told everybody for days what a great hunter I was going to be. But I lost interest in all of that as I grew older. I didn't really enjoy killing animals, but more than that, hanging out with my buddies and doing drugs was more important than spending time with him. Besides, we'd have lots of time for that stuff when the party years were over.

Wherever we were going in the car, Dad would always pickup hitchhikers – mostly Native ones, mostly drunk Native ones, to be honest! I used to hate having to put up with them until they got out. He would just laugh! Dad had a deep love for Aboriginal Canadians. It all goes back to where he grew up: a little town called Spanish, Ontario, off the North Channel of Georgian Bay. He lived close to a lot of Natives and hunted and played sports with them all the time. They were family to him, so much so, that from all the stories I heard, I thought I was native, too. I ended up telling my 3rd grade teacher that I was part Indian. She looked at my blonde hair, blue eyes and tried to look like she believed me. She ended up asking my sister, Sharon, who was teaching at the same school, about it. Needless to say, they had a good laugh over it.

The older I got, the more our relationship became limited to the garage. I worked with my Dad every day, and came to respect him as a kind and generous, Christian gentleman. Everybody is looking for an honest mechanic. My dad was more than that. He would help you any way he could. Getting up in the middle of the night to help a stranded motorist was nothing unusual for Tommy Moore, and he would never think of asking anything for it either.

One day while working on a truck at the shop, Dad cut his head wide open. I mean, wi-i-i-de open! It seemed like I could almost see his brains. I tried to get him to go to the hospital, but he was too stubborn for that. He said he would sit down for awhile and he would be okay (as blood was pouring down his face). Finally he agreed that maybe he should get a doctor to look at it. We arrived at the hospital and were quickly rushed into an emergency examination room.

A nurse showed up and asked, "Are you Billy Moore?"

"Sure am," I said. She informed me that my wife Jean, had been rushed to the other hospital, and was about to have my baby. So I left Dad in Emerg, went to the other hospital and waited for my son Tyler to be born. One of the funniest snapshots I have is the one of Dad, with thirty-seven stitches in his head and two huge black eyes, holding newborn Tyler with a big smile on his face.

When my Mother died, my Dad was lost. I wasn't there emotionally for him at all. I worked every day with him but that was about it. But fortunately, Dad had someone else to turn to: Andy, the boarder I mentioned earlier, became the son my father used to have. He took the place I once held when I was young. He was there for him, and I know my Dad cared a lot for Andy. I thank Andy from the bottom of my heart for all of the help and support he gave my Dad.

A fairly short while later, my Father remarried. She was a good woman from the church and she had been a friend of my Mom's. At the time, I thought it was good for him. Truth was, I really thought it was good for me. After all, it soothed my guilt for not being there when he needed me! As time went on though, it became difficult on our family – especially Jean, Tyler and me, as we were the only immediate family in the same town. In the end when Dad died, it was a very bad scene, and I have to admit, I still have some resentment towards my Step-Mother, though I try not to.

To sum it all up, Tommy Moore was the best, and I really was a disappointment to him in so many ways. He used to ask my Mom, "Where did we go wrong?" I just didn't 'get it' until much later in life. I would love to go hunting with him today, if I could. You think that the people in your life will be there forever; that there's lots of time to make it up to them, but you're wrong. And when they're gone, they're gone for a long, long time.

Dad was in Florida when he got really sick. He had been sick for a few years after he had half of his stomach removed, but now it was serious. He was told to go home, and my sister Ardith, was given the difficult job of telling him that the doctors had given him two or three weeks to live. He made his last, long road trip back to Sudbury, full of cancer. He came back to town and went to see everyone he knew and loved to say goodbye. No one really believed him though, but he died just about when the doctors said he would. He was a tough man with a tender heart.

I remember sitting on the couch with him at my house a little while before he died, and telling him he was the best Dad anyone could ever have. Then he left to go to our camp on Manitoulin Island. We didn't believe he was really dying either. One night, I got a call to get up there, as he was in the hospital again. It had become routine, a few days in the hospital, then back home. I kind of took my time, and had a few beers on the way. When I got there, I asked the nurse at the front desk what room he was in. She paused, and said that the doctor wanted to see me. Immediately, I knew he was gone. Once I knew he was dead, I refused to see him. The pastor from the church on the Island was there, and he kept urging me and I almost told him where he could go. But instead, I turned around and drove back to Sudbury. That night, I got wasted.

Chapter 6:
Out of Control

And I continued to get wasted... daily.

After a few years of continuous use, I crossed the "invisible" line and became totally dependent on drugs and alcohol. I was an addict! It didn't happen on any particular day as if I woke up one frigid, February Friday and that was it. Instead, it just sort of snuck up on me and then I couldn't remember how long it had been since I had been this way.

I was an addict, but I never would have admitted it and I sure didn't know I was one. But there was not one day in the next twenty-seven years, that I was straight or sober. I just couldn't function without having my 'fix'. I was so bad that when I ran out of pot, I would call everyone I knew, friends of friends of friends, to find some. I literally couldn't function without it; without it my body cried out and my mind would go numb. No one knew I was stoned all of the time because they never saw me straight! The odd time when I actually tried to go without, even for a day, it would drive Jean crazy. Finally, she'd shove me out the door to get some because she couldn't stand me when I was straight.

Marijuana had become my drug of choice. I would drink as well, but alcohol wasn't something I abused at this point. I might drink, but not without a joint. Alcohol alone just didn't do it for me. Pot was what I craved; what I needed; it was my life support; my nirvana. Today you often hear people say that weed isn't a serious problem; that you don't get addicted to it. But I can tell you that you really can, and over the years, I have known people whose entire lives have been dominated by marijuana. When you're in this space, you can't cross the street without having a toke. You can't cope with the easiest decisions, or enjoy the simplest pleasures without a buzz. And when you're dealing with emotions or issues with your conscience, there's nothing like a joint to take the edge off; quiet the pangs and numb the heart. If that isn't 'addicted', I don't know what is. It's funny how people tell me that weed is harmless, but in the next sentence they tell me it's much stronger and more potent than it ever has been. Isn't that kind of an oxymoron? I sometimes challenge friends today to go without it for two weeks, and they tell me they could, but they just don't want to. I recognize that line, because it's what I used to tell my sister, Ardie, and it's a sure sign of problems.

During these years, I escaped death and injury many times. Often I drove while under the influence of drugs or alcohol. Miraculously, I was never charged by the police. I have no record! Sometimes when the police pulled me over, they would let me go because they were hockey buddies or they knew my wife, Jean, as she worked for headquarters. But in all those years, I never was arrested for DUI or busted for drugs. Sometimes I think about some of my close calls, and I realize that it wasn't just that I was saved, but I wonder how many people's lives were in danger because of my recklessness.

One night, Al and I were coming back from the Coulson Hotel, heavily under the influence of drugs and alcohol while driving my brand new Thunderbird Turbo Coupe the way it was supposed to be driven: fast. Unfortunately, I wasn't on a track and I was in no condition to handle speed. It was in the spring of that year on a cold, wet night. Of course, I was driving aggressively and I lost control and fishtailed on an icy bridge. Next thing, we were skidding violently one way, then the other as I fought to gain control. Then slow motion – freeze frame – the back end spun out, which caused the sound of crunching metal against the guardrail… we glided through the air until there was a dull thud… then silence… and then we returned to reality with the stereo blaring INXS!

At that moment, I was sitting in my car with its front end in the river. The car was badly damaged. Somehow, though, it started and I put it in reverse. Slowly, the wheels began to grip, and amazingly enough, we backed out of the water. My friend Al, got out and looked. I couldn't bear to do it. I was still hoping it wasn't too bad. He just shook his head and said, "It's pretty bad". I limped the car home with pieces falling off all the way and proceeded to tell Jean. SHE FREAKED!

I knew someone was watching over me, as we both walked away without a scratch – even though I wasn't wearing my seatbelt! Why wasn't I hurt or killed? I did the only thing I thought I had to: a lot of lying to the insurance company. Eventually, after a ton of cross-examination, they fixed the car and everything was okay. The car was as good as new and I learned a lesson. Never drive fast on that bridge!

In a similar situation, my close buddy, Brett, was not so fortunate. He was also my brother-in-law, and was actually working for me at the shop. We spent a lot of time together, hanging out, as well as playing hockey and ball together. Our birthdays were on the same day, and one birthday night, we went to my parents' house for dinner and later played hockey against each other. We travelled to the game together and got high on the way. I'll never forget that shutout: beating his team, 2-0.

Brett was also heavy into drugs and, straight or stoned, he was the craziest driver I ever knew. One night while under the influence and driving too fast on a narrow city street, he lost control of his car and hit a building. He was killed instantly. I was supposed to see him later that evening but I never saw him alive again! This had a major affect on Jean and I. Our marriage was never the same after that. Though we both mourned his death, we did it differently. Jean missed her little brother and I mourned for my party buddy. That's when my cocaine use began to escalate.

Brett's accident also had a devastating effect on Jean's family. I don't know how my in-laws did it – losing their baby. Jean was working at the police station that night. She was actually the dispatcher who took the call of the accident and recognized her brother's license. She called me to say that Brett had been in an accident and she would be home late because she had to go identify the body. I can still feel the pain I felt at that moment. We both did whatever we could to stop the pain.

For me, it was coke. I started hanging around with Brett's buddies, guys in their late twenties who were about ten years younger than me. There was Al, who later shared the T-Bird accident with me; and another Brett, who lived in a party house with him. Like me, they were trying to cope, too. They looked up to me and respected me – probably because of the Van and the shop, and maybe because I had a little money, too.

These guys knew how to party. There were always good-looking women and lots of dope and booze. I stopped hanging around all the guys my age because they were lame. When I played ball with my older friends, we'd all go out after the game. But after a few beers, Brian and the boys would go home to their wives and families. Not me though. A few beers with them just got me going, so I would have to hit the bars and never know where I would end up or what time I would get home.

So that was it – they were left in the dust. On the odd occasion, I could persuade Brian to come out with me, but his wife definitely hated it, and any time Brian came, it would be at great personal cost: administered by his wife, Alice.

At this point, I had the business to myself. I felt like I was on Easy Street. Jean and I were working things out. Tyler was a teenager and getting into his own stuff, and I was running the shop. Dad had sold it to me in a shrewd business deal for one dollar. Known as "the most honest shop" in town, I was thrilled to be on my own and a businessman. Of course, I didn't know what that included. I saw the money coming in – money to spend, money to party, money to impress my buddies – and I forgot the bills to be paid, especially the taxes to the government. But, I had so many friends to buy drinks for at the bar and so many parties to grace with my presence, and could I help it if the women were drawn, too? Everyone wanted me (and my money) around! I was into a new scene now, younger and wilder, and definitely more fun. I turned friends into strangers, and strangers into friends and I was on top of the world.

I had a lot of stuff, too. I had four trucks, three cars, a pretty cool boat, a nice house, and a cottage which I shared with my sister, Ardie. It had been my parents' cottage on Manitoulin Island. The best thing about the cottage was that living in Toronto, Ardie and John were busy with their own lives and didn't have much time for the seven hour drive to get there. That was fine with me, so Jean and I were there a lot, sometimes with Tyler and sometimes not. We had some great times... parties with all my friends, skiing and tubing on the lake, a little fishing and some volleyball or golf at Mindemoya. Oh yeah, and DRINKING and DOPING!

Everything I did revolved around drugs and alcohol. When I played hockey, I was always high, and we all drank a few before the game at the bar, as well as in the dressing room. I played with a lot of ex NHL'ers and they were pretty hard core. We even were league champions a few times; I don't know how we did it... except that maybe the other teams were just as wasted as we were.

I had begun to do some mud bogging. For you novices, it's like drag racing in a truck, only in the mud. I took one of my old 4x4's that I had used to plow snow with, and ran it in the stock class. I won 2nd place in the first race I ever entered. I was hooked. This began a new addiction or obsession. I sank more and more money into the truck to make it look cooler and go faster, and it did. Eventually, I had a 454 cubic inch engine with 600 horsepower and it was quick, to say the least. Of course I had a few tokes and a few beers before every race, and sometimes a few lines, although it was against the rules. After every event, we would collect the hardware and prize money and head to the beer tent for a few more ales, then load up the trailer and drive home wasted.

We went all over Ontario racing every weekend we could. Once we were travelling on the 144, a two-lane and very narrow highway on our way home from a race in Hearst. It was the middle of the night and I was towing my race truck on a trailer. A transport truck coming from the other direction got so close to me that it broke my driver's side mirror off with a loud smash! That was close – too close! Of course, we were drunk – so I can't really be sure which of us was on the wrong side of the road!

One day, out of the blue, I got a letter from the RCMP to say that my phone had been tapped for the last month. I freaked! What did I say? And to whom? Was I in trouble? I didn't have a clue what it was about, though I guessed it could have something to do with drugs. The day after Super Bowl Sunday, I came home at noon – a hurting unit – after a late night of who knows what. The Mounties were at the house waiting for me and took me down to headquarters for questioning. It turned out that they were interested in my involvement with a certain dealer who was suspected of some shady business out West. It didn't help that he was my dealer, and I had borrowed a significant amount of money for the business from him. After a few hours of interrogation, playing good cop/bad cop, they let me go. They threatened me to talk, or Jean could lose her job with the police. But I figured they were bluffing and trying to get me to rat out my friend. I honestly didn't know his personal business. Finally, they let me go but, as the song by Buffalo Springfield says, "Paranoia, it strikes deep". I found myself looking over my shoulder for weeks afterward and watched myself very closely after that. Of course, the whole thing upset Jean (as her job was in jeopardy), so she was on my case. It scared me too, but it wasn't long before all was back to normal; I buried the situation in a joint, a line, or the bottom of a bottle.

The pressures of not knowing how to run a business were getting to me and I didn't have the tools to cope with it. One night after coming home drunk, I had an argument with my wife about money. She hated the fact that we had money problems from time to time. We were in the upstairs bedroom and I was getting angrier and angrier. Finally, in a fit of frustration and rage, I went out on the balcony and jumped off. I was in mid-air when I realized what I'd done. I actually remember thinking to myself in that split second, "Uh-oh, this is going to hurt!" It was 16-18 feet down and I was in bare feet. I landed heavily on my heels and crushed them both. My knee came up to smash me in the chin. I bit my tongue, and started bleeding and then I was out cold. When I was finally alert, I lay there waiting for help, but nobody came. Of course, the only one who knew about it was Jean, and she wasn't too interested. I seemed to pull these kinds of stunts every once in awhile, hoping someone (Jean, I suppose) would hear my cry and rescue me.

On another occasion after another drunken fight, I pulled out my Dad's hunting rifle and held it to my head, hoping Jean would stop me. I was pretty sure it wasn't loaded, but when you're in that state, who knows what can happen? I pulled the trigger and… nothing. And no one came to my rescue that time, either. Jean didn't come running to stop me; she didn't try to save me from myself, and I slid just a little lower down the tube. Of course, now I wonder what was going on in her head. Would I come after her with that rifle? Would I shoot her? Would I hurt Tyler? When I think of it now, I feel awful for the mental misery I must have put my family through.

But, back to the great leap into the darkness. I remained on the ground for a long while until I finally decided no one was coming. So, on my hands and knees, I dragged myself into the house and onto a couch where I lay in total agony for two days. Jean just went about her business, simply ignoring me. I guess I had really shown her! Finally my buddy, Brett, came and took me to the doctor.

My foolishness left my feet damaged for life. Was it a cry for help? As I look back knowing what I know now, it definitely was. I crawled around on all fours for about a month before I could even put enough weight on my feet to use crutches. I still, to this day, have a lot of problems and have to wear very expensive orthotics to get any relief. They seem to get worse every year. Some things you pay for on the long-term installment plan.

During those years, there were lots of folks around me willing and ready to help. Whenever one of them approached me, I would try to put on a happy face and let on that all was well. The only help I needed was a little extra cash. People loved me, cared for me, worried about me and prayed for me, but I refused or ignored their help. It would mean I had to straighten out and I didn't need to do that! Everything would work out okay... or at least that's what I told myself.

Ardith's Story

Bill and his friends would go to the Molson Indy every year and stay at my place in Toronto. Some years, we would be away and only Wade, my son would be home. After Bill left, Wade informed me that he and his friends were using a lot of drugs, including cocaine. I did see some burn holes in my floor after their visit. I advised Sharon and we drove down from Manitoulin Island to confront Bill. He denied using cocaine and was furious at Wade for telling me.

My sister, Ardith, had remarried and moved back to Toronto. I went to visit her a few times a year. Her new husband, John, who was a doctor, liked to drink as well so I felt right at home there. My buddies and I would stay there every summer when we went to the Molson Indy. That was just a big three-day drinking marathon for us. Ardith knew enough about alcohol from her husband, and was beginning to notice the signs of imminent disaster in my life. She could see the train wreck coming. So, when things started to unravel, she was willing to get me help. But I wasn't ready yet! I hadn't hit bottom yet! A few years later, when I was ready, she was very supportive of me in many ways. I remain in close contact with her today, and we still get together quite often. Ardie never stops telling me how proud she is of me, because she saw me at my worst.

Eventually, the bill collectors came calling! I didn't know what to do! I put them off as long as I could! I've always been a good mechanic, but I never claimed to be a savvy business-man – especially at that time, when credit meant instant cash and cash meant longer and better binges. So phone calls were ignored; mail was left unopened. Then the government came to call and I knew that I needed help.

All this time, I was smoking up every couple of hours and getting drunk every night, just to cope with the pressures of life and business. What could I do? I was running out of options!

Sharon dropped into the shop to have a short visit. I never, ever called her, as she and her family were all Christians and I felt uncomfortable and embarrassed around them – but now she had come to me. Knowing I needed her help, I braced myself for whatever compromises I'd have to make to get it. I asked to speak with her in the office. That's when I told her the mess I was in but not the reason for it! Being the "big sister", she said that she would see what she could do to help.

This started another chapter in my life. She moved into our home for a week and the first thing she did was open 6 months' worth of mail – mostly bills. I promised her I would quit pot if she could help me. Once she saw where I was at financially, she arranged a large personal loan and co-signed for me. All this was done with my full agreement. At this point, I truly believed that if I had help with the business, I could turn my life around. Little did I know how addicted I really was and what a turnaround would actually mean.

For awhile, all went well. I went to her place on Manitoulin Island for a week and went off pot – cold turkey. I locked myself in a room at their cottage. I had a ton of movies and Ardie, the nurse, gave me some sleeping pills. I slept and watched movies for 3 days, I think, before I even came out for something to eat. Then, back in for a few more days. It was rough and I wouldn't suggest anyone try this, but Sharon and Ken were monitoring me to make sure things didn't get too hairy. After a week, I got over the physical withdrawals, but there was still a long way to go. When I left their place with tears and vows and lots of good vibes, I actually thought I had it licked. Things were turning around! I was on the downhill slope now!

But on the way home, actually, before I even got off the Island, I thought like any good addict: I should reward myself. So I stopped for a six-pack of beer. I drank them as I was turning a new leaf on my way home to the good life. Beer didn't really do the trick, but in the absence of marijuana, it was starting to taste pretty good. Things – I thought – were looking up.

Sharon would take care of business at the shop, and I would do the work. It was a good deal on paper. At first, she drove into the garage every second day to oversee matters. But the drive from Kagawong on Manitoulin to Sudbury was 120 miles each way, and since things seemed to be on the up and up, she started to come twice a week and then once a week. Sharon handled all the money (except what I hid from her so I could have a few beers) and she paid all the bills. For the next two years the shop was on track. And Sharon thought I was, too.

But that's when the drinking really kicked in, and I hid it from Sharon as much as possible. The less often she came, the more I hit the bottle and now I was starting to use cocaine more than ever. After all, I only promised to quit smoking pot – and I did! But behind the pot was a deeper problem – the maze of co-dependency. I realize now that I just switched addictions and my body was more than happy I did. Over time, it latched onto alcohol just as it had to grass, and soon, that became my new drug of choice. It was like moving to the next level in a video game – same old problems, new thrills.

And with these changes, my marriage fell on hard times! Jean had known me for 20 years as a pothead. She didn't like it, but we had found a certain accommodation. I was a laid-back, easy-going, largely unmotivated, couch potato. Not the best of husbands, but generally pliable. But when these new addictions took over, I morphed into an aggressive, angry, hyper dude looking for a fight. Not that I was a street fighter by any means, but I was now a little more pumped for a brawl with Jean. And brawl we did – at the drop of a hat. Things never got physical, but it wasn't pretty and Jean was starting to get to the end of her rope with me.

Eventually, everything began to fall apart all over again. With my new addictions, I spent more and more time at the bar and less and less time at home. Of course, it took increasing amounts of money to fund my new life. I got that from cheating my sister. When she would pick up the cash from a week's business, it would always be after I had skimmed enough off the top to bankroll Billy's Fun House. The scam was simple: I would work to earn an agreed upon quota – then everything else I made, I took in cash and never told Sharon about it.

On Canada Day, 1996, my buddies and I were putting them back at my favourite hang-out, the Nickel City. Bobby, Jerry and Craig and I were watching videos of me mud-racing in a truck called UFO-454. And we were getting very drunk, too. Feeling insufficiently wrecked and needing a second wind, I decided to go buy an 8 ball of coke (3.5 grams). I always carried what became known as "my paper wallet". It was a white envelope with all the money from the shop in it. I was supposed to deposit it in the bank the day before, but I got side-tracked at the bar. Anyway, it had about $900 in it, and so what if I blew $200 of it on coke? Only problem was, when I got to my dealer's house and went to pay for the coke, I had no money! I had lost it! I retraced my steps – but to no avail – it was gone for good. I was livid! So I did the only thing I could do: I went to the shop, wrote a check to myself for $200 and cashed it at the bar. Then I went back to the dealer's house and bought my 8 ball. Insanity or what? Now I was behind $1,100, not just $200. The solution? Work like a mad man for cash under the table until I made enough to pay Sharon off so she wouldn't find out.

That strategy couldn't work forever. The deeper I got into coke and flashed my coin for all my buddies to see, the deeper the hole got at work. Sharon saw it coming before I did and she tried to warn me, but as usual, I knew better. I was in further than I thought. One parts supplier started demanding payment, and even though I tried to work out a deal with him, he wanted every cent right now. Instead, he got nothing. I looked into bankruptcy and discovered that for a small fee, I could free myself once more and start out with yet another clean slate. Since the business was now in Sharon's name and nothing I owned was in mine, it turned out that bankruptcy would have no immediate consequences, except to stiff the jerk that was on my case. So I did it. The shop that was once called Crossing Alignment shut down one day and opened the next as Bill's Crossing Alignment. Abracadabra, all my problems were gone again.

Eventually though, I saw the bankruptcy for what it was: another ruse to keep me away from reality. As long as I could avoid the harsh light of responsibility and live in the smoke and mirrors of fresh starts, bailouts, the seductive escape of cocaine and the oblivion of alcohol, everything was going to be alright.

Drugs scrambled every part of my life. Relationships with anyone were never what they seemed. Cocaine really messed me up in the area of sex. I think I was addicted there, too. It was a coping mechanism for when I felt pain. Sex was just an avenue of escape to make me feel good about myself and forget everything for awhile. And cocaine was a lot like sex in the same way. Someone told me coke makes your brain feel like it's having an orgasm – he was right. The only problem is, when you come down off of coke, you hate yourself for spending all that money and doing the things you did. It's all kind of foggy but I did many things while "high" that I am totally ashamed of now that my mind is clear. It was a very dark time for me. I know God has forgiven me and that it's all behind me, but sometimes it still haunts me. I guess it's hard to forgive myself.

But Jean didn't forgive me! She wanted out. She needed out. She had to get away from me before I dragged her down with me. She told me that she didn't love me anymore, and that we had to split up for good. It all came down the same day I declared bankruptcy. What I saw as a clean slate, she recognized as the next step in a recurring pattern of irresponsibility.

I figured we would get back together in awhile, because that's what we always did. But this time was different – there was someone else! Even after I found out, I still thought it was temporary... but it wasn't. In a way, I didn't care. They deserved each other! She'll come crawling back after he slaps her around a bit. Besides, I'm invincible. Things get rough at times, but they always work out. I'm a big shot! I've got lots of money now with no more creditors on my back... I've got good friends who love to party, and my sister is always a phone call away to straighten things out! So who needs her anyway? I'm a free man and no one can tell me what to do anymore. My Mom and Dad are gone; Brett is gone and so is Jean; at 18, Tyler's got his own life to live, and I don't need anybody!

Was I feeling left behind and all alone again? One thing I didn't know was that all that pain was just being stored in the bottom of a bottle, and it would come back eventually. So the choice I made that winter night – years earlier – to experiment with drugs and alcohol didn't come without a price; little did I know, the downward spiral was just beginning.

Chapter 7:
Losing the Business

Sharon's Story:

As Bill continued to deteriorate, my concern grew. I prayed and prayed but nothing seemed to change. The problems went on and on! One day as I was walking and praying and crying, it was as though God spoke to me… in my head I heard, "It will be okay." I thought, "Okay?", but then I heard again, "No, OK!"

We had just finished an acrostic on P-R-A-Y-E-R in our Bible Study group. As I began to mull over okay as an acrostic, it came to me (in the words of songs we sang at church):

> *O – Only believe,*
> *Only believe,*
> *All things are possible*
> *Only believe.*

> *K – Keep on believing,*
> *God will answer prayer.*
> *Keep on believing,*
> *Never despair.*
> *When you are heavy laden*
> *And burdened down with care,*
> *Remember God still loves you*
> *And He'll answer your prayer.*

They were old songs we'd sung for years, but now something came alive in those words. I felt that I couldn't "believe". How could God straighten out Bill's life? But, I held on to the 'okay promise' and kept singing those two choruses over and over whenever I became discouraged.

And God DID answer – but not right away!

So here I am, as far as anybody knew, a fairly successful business man, with assets. Okay, I had a few minor setbacks, but it was all good now. I was an eligible bachelor; I had a cool apartment for me and my dog Winston, who was my best and most loyal friend (even if I didn't feed him regularly!). I had some lady friends to go out with when I wanted – you might call them 'friends with benefits'. There were always my buddies Bobby, Jerry and Craig at the bar to drink with.

It's funny how my crowd changed a little, when I stopped smoking pot. I hung around with drinkers mostly now. I still wasn't smoking pot because of my promise but, of course, I did coke regularly and I was becoming addicted to it, although I would never admit it. After all, I could afford it! Jean was gone for good and would show up occasionally at my bar with her new man. That killed me! But I guess what goes around comes around.

Then I met Ellen. Everyone said to stay away from her – she's bad news. And she did have a reputation of sorts. We saw each other a few times and I tried to keep my distance, but I was lured in with sex, drugs, and rock and roll. Ellen quickly stole my heart, along with her four little kids and her ample bosom. Before long, it seemed we had become a family.

I was spending a lot of time at Ellen's during the day when I should have been at the shop. Occasionally, we would take off for a few days here and there. Bottom line: I wasn't making it to work much. Instead I was enjoying the good life: making money without putting in the hours. I would go into Crossing to make sure all was well, take some money and leave. I had left a guy named Paul in charge. We had worked together for ten years. I had given Paul his first job as a mechanic, and now he had worked his way up to management. I trusted Paul, especially because I paid him so well. So things were good. What could possibly go wrong? I couldn't have dreamed it in my wildest dreams.

Ellen turned my life upside down. I became totally dependent on her and I loved her four little kids. By now, my old van-building buddy, Ernie, had moved into the apartment with me. But, in fact, I was staying at Ellen's most of the time and helping her out a lot financially. Very soon, the party-hearty Billy was gone and a new, gentler, more domesticated Billy appeared. I took care of the kids, I did the laundry, I washed the dishes and did the housework – anything to keep the little woman happy. It's not that I stopped snorting and drinking; it's just that I had lost interest in doing it with anyone but Ellen.

It's hard to define what our relationship was, if there really was one at all. We were part-time lovers and full-time stoners. There was sex, but there was a lot of drinking and doping, too. I had managed to stay away from marijuana for a number of years until Ellen came along. A toke here and there became a joint now and again, and next thing, I was back to where I started, but with alcohol and cocaine added to the mix. Beyond that, though, we didn't really have much of a rapport. It's not like we became soul mates or fellow travelers. Truth be told, I never trusted her.

She was a great story-teller, and she had me hook, line and sinker a lot of the time. Though she really did come from a pretty uppity background, she told me tale after tale of running her own business and owning her own apartment building, and still here I was pouring my own money in to keep us afloat. I found out it was hard to believe anything she said, and I just couldn't bring myself to confront her about it.

She bounced me up and down like a yo-yo, and I would just let her. Sometimes she would tell me she was going out to see a friend and leave me babysitting her kids. She would take off in my truck and would come home at 2:00 a.m. in the morning with a drunk or two who thought they were coming in for the night. I recognized the scam for what it was, because that's how I got caught up with Ellen in the first place. The difference now was that I wouldn't end up like the poor chump who gave up his place in her bed for me! So I would get up and entertain them with a few beers until I could make sure they were out of the house.

To this day, I can't figure out how I got in this messed-up relationship. The only thing I can say about it is something I learned in recovery: sick people attract sick people, and that's what both of us were. She had me wound around her finger and I let her do that, because I needed her to make me happy!

One night, after we were out with the kids, we pulled in the driveway and there was a sign hanging from the basketball net. I went to look at it and it said, "Mark thanks you for the weekend with Ellen." What the – what was this? Ellen didn't say much of anything. I asked and asked until she just locked me out and told me to go home. I pounded on the door looking for an explanation, but she just picked up the phone and said, "If you don't get out of here, I'm calling the cops." I knew she would, so I left.

On my way home, and all that sleepless night, I started putting it together. A couple of weeks ago, I had been in a ball tournament, so the whole team spent a wild night at one of the guy's camps down at the French River. With nothing else to do, Ellen asked if she could take the truck to a fishing derby out by Sturgeon Falls. While she was out there, she said she decided to stay overnight because she didn't want to drive my truck drunk. At least, that's what she had said.

Now I was thinking different. After all, the fishing derby was at a guy named Mark's camp, and wasn't that the guy's name on the sign? And hadn't she gone to a wedding a few weeks earlier and mentioned that she'd met up with this old friend, Mark? It was all coming together in my slow, drug-addled mind. The whole thing was a lie! She had spent that wedding night with Mark while I looked after her kids, and as I began piecing other past mysteries together, it occurred to me that this fishing excursion wasn't the first time! I was devastated!

The pain I experienced over the loss of Ellen was uncontrollable. I couldn't eat; I couldn't sleep (unless I was drunk) and work became impossible. I couldn't concentrate for one second. I just stayed home, sitting in my rocking chair, drinking and waiting for her to call or come over. I wanted her back, BAD! I had the scenario playing out in my mind. She would call to apologize. She would beg for forgiveness and tell me that no one had ever treated her better than I did and she was a fool to treat things with me that lightly. Was there any way I would take her back? I would take her in my arms, rub away the tears and kiss her passionately. Of course, I'd forgive her because she was the one true love of my life; we would walk out into the sunset to do lines and drink tequila, happily ever after. Meanwhile, Ernie would shake his head at me and say with a scowl, "You idiot… I told you to stay away from her in the first place!"

After about a week, she showed up to try to console me. Then she began dropping over at my place now and then, saying things to keep my hopes up and I fell for it. She'd come by, she would seduce me – and things would be nice for a day or two – then she'd be gone. After awhile, it became clear that I was the fall back position when things weren't going so well with Mark.

In the middle of all this soap opera stuff, things started to fall way behind with Sharon again. They had gone from bad to worse over the length of my nine months with Ellen, but now, though Sharon had been threatening me all along with ultimatums, the situation was officially desperate. I was missing the loan payments and she had to pay them. "That's okay," I would tell myself. "I'll make it up next month." But next month never came, and I got further and further behind.

This went on for a few more months and finally something happened that I never, ever could have imagined in a million years! Sharon wrote me a letter just before Christmas of 1998, and told me she had sold the business to Paul, my manager and friend, as of January 1, 1999. This was an all-time low! How could they do this to me? And behind my back! Of course, it was all her fault! I was just getting it together! I remember my brother-in-law telling me that one day I would thank them for closing me down and selling to Paul. But not today! I was angry, furious and hurt! I resented what she had done and I hated Paul! After all I had done for him! I paid him a lot of money to take care of the place and look at what he does to me!

I felt that the rug was pulled out from under me when I wasn't expecting it! She had warned and warned me, and now for fear of losing all she had invested, Sharon decided it was time to get something out of Dad's business instead of excuses. Somehow, I thought things could just go on and on and one day all would be well. How could they not understand? Well, if that's how your own sister can treat you, I was done with both her and Paul for good! Stupid Christians and their stupid Christian self-righteousness!

Sharon's Story:

During those messy years of helping Bill and lending him more and more money on his "promise" of soon repayment, I was becoming more and more upset. Chest pains and headaches were becoming common. These were rarely felt before and I was afraid that I was going to have a heart attack!

One night, as I was tossing and turning as usual and praying about the situation, I heard a voice. Whether it was audible or in my head, I can't tell you. The voice said, "It's only money!" I realized that it was the Lord so I replied, "Yes, Lord, but it's a lot of money!" Again I heard, "It's only money!" With that, I turned over and went to sleep – the first solid sleep in a long time. The pain left and I've been fine ever since.

This did not ease our money problems, but I was no longer anxious. We continued to pay $1,500 a month for the next three years until the debt was finally cleared! That final payment was a glorious day, as it took all of my pension every month for those three years. God was good and we always had what we needed. This taught us many *lessons, especially that we could live on much less and we could be more generous to other ministries and the needy. This lesson, we have put into practice.*

As things went from bad to worse, I knew I would be okay as long as I had my beer, my rocking chair and my TV – and as long as my dog Winston still loved me! Truth be told, the tank was empty. I was emotionally, physically, psychologically and spiritually spent. There was nothing left. I had been running on fumes and now even that was gone – and frankly, I didn't care! The whole world was against me: friends, family, anyone in my path. They all wanted to see me fail, so now they could gloat all they wanted! They had wrecked my life and it was all their fault and NOT mine! They thought I was bad before? They hadn't seen anything yet!

I wanted everyone to feel sorry for me – but nobody did. I was desperately lonely. Wasn't anyone going to come bail me out this time? I was a boat full of holes, and I was sinking fast. There had always been someone around to keep me afloat before. But now I was all alone. I knew I was going down, and I needed to plug the holes. But how? I needed help! But I wasn't ready for it just yet.

I don't know how I survived after both the garage and Ellen were gone. I had sold my Thunderbird to a friend and those funds were supposed to make my truck payments for the next while. For a number of years, I supported my illicit activities by snow plowing through the winter, and I still had a good fifty contracts that would keep me in drugs and alcohol for the season. At this point, though, as I was hitting the skids, it was mostly alcohol since it was cheaper, and it actually numbed me out so I didn't have to think. It was a good winter for snow, so I would get up at 4:00 a.m., have a few beers and go plowing. Driving within inches of parked vehicles while completely drunk was routine, and although I had done it for years, I never, ever hit one! After my route was done, I would head to the bar and drink until I had to lie down or ran out of money for the day!

One night at the Nickel City Hotel, I was drowning my sorrows and sharing my tale of woe with anyone who would listen. I think it got old for a lot of people real quick, so I was always on the hunt for a new drinking partner. This particular evening, Ellen showed up at the same bar and I thought I'd have a drink with her, but it turned out she had other plans. After getting the cold shoulder for awhile, I decided to leave – why ruin my night with her nonsense? As I hopped into my plowing truck to leave, I noticed that she had come in a car that I had bought with my own money, which was still registered, licensed, and insured in my name. I started to leave when I got this great idea: I'll just ding her car as I go. You know, nothing like a little revenge to make one's self feel better. But when I shifted gears, I just saw red and smashed right into it. The whole car buckled as I tore across it from rear to front, crushing the driver's door altogether as I left.

It was a dark time, and as the shadows deepened to consume my soul, I could feel myself slipping from reality. It seemed as though I had walked into the Northern Brewery Beer Store on Lorne Street, one cold January morning, and came out with a bottomless case of beer. For five months, day in and day out, I drank myself to oblivion. I couldn't eat or sleep. I cried like a baby every night for those months. I suppose I was waiting for some kind of miracle or something – but it never came. Was this the end of the rope? Could things get any worse?

Bottoming Out... At Last

Every morning started the same way... with my head in the toilet, puking out whatever was in my stomach. This had been going on for about a year. I would start to retch, get to the porcelain god and make my morning offering. I had actually convinced myself that this was normal. Everybody – at least real guys – did life this way.

I'd get up, usually on the couch after a sleepless night, shaking like a leaf; chills running through my whole body. Even my vision was blurry and of course, there was the dry heaving. But I knew the cure – I just needed my "medicine"! Somehow a couple of beers or a few tokes would do the trick, and I'd be feeling a whole lot better soon enough. My stomach would settle, the shakes would stop and I was ready to begin my day.

Life at this point wasn't too complicated, but it pretty well overwhelmed me, most days. It consisted of watching talk shows all morning, waiting for Ellen to come over (which she actually did from time to time) and then going to hang out at the bar. And, of course, to keep the symptoms away, I had to resort to the "medicine" every two hours or so. It made me feel better by making it so I didn't feel at all. That way, I didn't have to think about what a mess my life was, or face up to my failures, or grasp the fact that I was going down – and fast.

I didn't want to be like this – living each day the same. I spent most of my time alone or talking to old rubbies at the bar. The more I looked into those grey lifeless eyes, the more I saw myself (if I lived to be that old). I wanted to die, but I was afraid to because I knew where I would go – so life just went on. My body had become physically addicted and totally dependent on drugs and alcohol; anything mood-altering, just to escape, to feel "normal" was what I needed. Increasingly, though, beer became my drug of choice. It took away the pain – and unlike drugs – it also numbed my mind. I could actually stop thinking about the mess I was in. I started to like beer a lot. When I had to choose between food and alcohol, it was alcohol every time!

Whose fault was this disaster? It sure wasn't mine! Who could I blame? I definitely hated Sharon and Ken. They had been behind my financial ruin! And I hated Paul for buying the shop right from under me. I hated Jean for betraying me and taking up with another guy, and leaving me alone. And while there were moments that I hated Ellen, I mostly longed for her, even though she was the most toxic person in my life. Funny how your judgment can become so skewed. The people who love you the most, you treat like trash and those who abuse you the most, you end up craving like a drug.

I was in a tailspin. Things were bad! I was so vulnerable and it felt like everywhere I turned, all I got was another kick in the groin. It was as though I had a sign around my neck that said, "PUNISH ME, I deserve it." And people did. They say that predators, like lions, can sense the weakest member of the herd and track it down as prey. I was becoming that victim. I had never been in a fight before, but twice during that period, just minding my own business, I got in a fight. Well, it wasn't much of a fight; I was just more of a punching bag. No family to turn to, no woman, nobody. Everyone had heard it before, and now they were just sick of me.

I had said to myself that I would really show them all how bad I could get. So I did, but I really didn't get any reaction.

Nobody cared anymore. I was a failure; a complete loser. I couldn't look anyone in the eye anymore. In fact, I just wanted to avoid people altogether. I went to the doctor for help and he gave me some antidepressants. They might have been helpful, but I never really found out. All I discovered is what a lethal combination they were with alcohol.

That's when the blackouts started. I was still living with Ernie in those days, and sometimes he would tell me what I did the night before, but I couldn't recall a thing. One morning, I got up looking for beer – hoping to cut short the daily ritual over the toilet. When there was none, I dragged myself to the truck and went out to get a six-pack. I was feeling a little weird, a little disconnected. I stopped at a cross street, and looking to see if there was any traffic, I realized that I couldn't see anything. It's not that I was blind or in such a stupor that I couldn't see, it's just that I looked out on Regent Street and drew a blank. My eyes refused to tell my brain what I was seeing. Now I was scared. I mean, I couldn't even trust my own senses anymore. So I turned the corner, crawled at a snail's pace to the beer store, not really sure where I was going or who was on the road. I bought my beer and cracked one open as soon as I got in the truck. I'm not sure how I got home, but I holed up for the day, frightened and alone.

I actually thought I was going crazy. Ellen would pop in and out of my life and tell me she loved me, and then I would see her at the bar with her new man. One time, both Jean and Ellen were at the bar with their new guys and it just about killed me. I knew exactly what was going on. They were laughing at me from across the smoky room and thinking, "I'm glad I got away from that loser... Just look at him!" I was once a King in that bar, and now here I was – a miserable shell of a man – being laughed at in his despair. It was all too much. I shut people out, and for two weeks, I went without eating and couldn't sleep for more than a few minutes at a time. I was unshaven, unwashed and wore the same rumpled clothing for days. I looked at myself in the mirror and saw those grey, lifeless eyes that I used to pity looking back at me. I had given up. It was over. I was now at rock bottom.

Maybe I was out of my mind. So I went to the local psychiatric hospital, the Sudbury Sanatorium. If I was crazy, I'd better talk to somebody about it. I signed myself in and saw some very sick people. I couldn't be that bad, could I? After a day of walking the halls and rubbing shoulders with people that were really mentally ill, I felt their pain. I finally saw a shrink, told him all my problems, and you know what he said? "You have a drinking problem. Fix that first, then we'll see if you're crazy." What a relief! So I went straight to the bar and had a few beers, thankful that I wasn't crazy, and heedless of the pressing problem of addiction. Besides, an addiction isn't as bad as being crazy. They lock you up when you're crazy! I was sure that I could deal with the addictions on my own!

As winter turned into spring, the big snow storms passed and snow plowing could no longer tie me over. My sources of income had dried up and borrowing twenty bucks here and there was getting old with anybody who knew me. I hadn't paid my apartment rent for awhile, so I was given my notice of eviction! My landlord had been a friend of mine and I kept telling him that I would pay, but then, 'this happened', or 'that happened", and I never did. He finally kicked me out and, like everyone else, made it clear he was very angry with me.

No one loved me; no one wanted me; even I hated the person I had become. So one night on the way home from the Nickel City, I decided to drive full speed into a wall at the Caruso

Club near my old garage. Everyone would always remember me that way – just like they remembered the corner where Brett died! I sped down Whittaker Street and headed straight at the wall. I kept accelerating until, at the last moment, I hit the brakes and skidded sideways, just barely making the turn up Haig Street, without crashing. I changed my mind in a split second! Could it have been God?

I had no money and nowhere to go. Was living on the street next? I had to give my dog, Winston, away because I couldn't keep him – but the guy I gave him to, passed him on to someone else, and I never saw him again! Winston was with me every day. He would come to the shop with me, go plowing with me – whatever I did, and wherever I went, he was there. Everyone knew him. He even came to the bar with me a few times. On my worst days, I had to admit that I neglected him. One day, just before I was evicted, I lay on the couch crying about the mess I was in. Winston hopped up on my chest, put his paws around my neck, and licked my tears! He forgave me! Then he became another one of those precious things I had lost because of my addiction.

Chapter 8:
Turning It Around

On eviction day, both Ernie and I had to leave the apartment. They threw me out because I hadn't paid a few months rent. They threw Ernie out because I had spent his rent money on booze. I knew I'd burnt him, and he did too. But a couple of days before we had to get out, Ernie put his arms around me and told me that he cared about me, and that I needed to get help. He knew of a place that his girlfriend, Norma, had gone to; a place that had really helped her. It was a Drug and Alcohol Treatment Centre in Elliot Lake, Ontario.

With nowhere else to go – and rock bottom kicking at my butt – I actually thought about it. I was seeing this lady, Denise, at the time – a woman, it seemed, even more broken than me. She had spent some time in AA, and she thought I should check it out. I figured I'd give it a try. So, without any plan in place, or even a phone call to the Centre, we headed off in my truck. Of course, we stopped a number of times to have a few drinks. After all, I couldn't do this sober! Besides, I would only be there a couple of weeks – they would give me a magic pill, I would feel great, the pain would be gone and everything would be fixed in my life… right?

Eventually, we made it to Elliot Lake sometime in the evening. The only building open at the Centre was Detox. I had no clue what to expect. I suppose I thought it was a cross between checking into a hotel and going to the hospital. I'd just show up, they'd put me up on the hoist in one of the open bays, fix me up, and send me on my way.

Denise came in with me. I approached the front desk. The guy looked up at me and said, "Yeah."

And out it came: "I'm a mess. I need help."

The guy did a double take. "What?"

"I'm a mess. I need help." That's the point where my life began to change! I didn't know that there were waiting lists everywhere for people to get help; I just knew I needed it immediately! I didn't realize that a lot of people were 'regular customers' brought to the Detox Centre by the cops – against their will. I wasn't aware that Detox was the first step for anybody before they could go to the Centre and that you had to jump through hoops to get in (because space was limited). All I knew was that I needed help. And that's why the intake worker did the double take. Not too many people just show up and admit they're fried, and that they need help.

The guy let me in and explained to me that he couldn't make any promises, but that I could stay for a few days. "We'll talk when you sober up," he said.

I said goodbye to Denise, not knowing what I was getting into. But I knew that I was at the point where the pain of getting better was going to be less than the pain I was in right now!

I spent the first night in the observation room. It's a room with three glass walls and four beds, right beside the front desk. It's like Grand Central Station! Nobody comes in or out without seeing you. I felt like an animal in a cage. Other clients walk by wondering, "Who's the new meat today?" Of course, they put you here so they can see you (in case of an emergency). But it was hell. I don't think I slept a wink; my pain was so immense. I couldn't stop thinking, how did I get here, how could this happen to me? Not to mention, I needed a drink to do this!

The Detox Centre took me in for a quick dry-out, but told me there was no way for me to get into the 28-day program I needed. I ended up staying in that facility for seven or eight days and went through painful withdrawals. Time went so slowly; the clock seemed like it was moving backwards. I couldn't sleep, and they wouldn't give me pills to help, although the doctor on staff gave us this drink that was supposed to ease the withdrawals. It started with four portions a day, and weaned down to just one on the last day. It really worked, but most of us began to crave the medicine instead.

I remember just sitting and staring out the window for hours at a time and going for long walks. I took about five whirlpools a day just to escape a little, but nothing helped. It was like bugs crawling inside your skin trying to get out; you'd get the chills and then hot flashes, and no matter what position you took – sitting or lying down – you were in agony. All you could think about was the pain – both the physical torment and the mental anguish. Your mind is racing through scrap books of memory: regret, remorse, shame, and the unremitting accusation that you and you alone are the author of your own demise. I couldn't bear to be with people, but I couldn't stand being alone. And it went on like that for days.

It was horrible! I would sit and talk with others going through the same stuff, and met some very interesting people from all walks of life. As I started to come through the worst of cold turkey, I began to sense a connection with these people: nurses, truck drivers, businessmen and housewives.

Most of them had been forced because of their actions to come, whether by family or business, but mainly through the courts; a few like me had simply come to the end of the rope and had nowhere else to turn. Somehow, though our stories were different as night and day, we shared the same pain. Addiction doesn't care who you are, or where you come from. Top of the heap or bottom of the barrel, it's an equal opportunity curse, and anybody can be a candidate.

I went to my very first AA meeting during my stay there. The first few days, they simply offered the meetings and I opted out, but eventually it was clear I had no choice. So I walked into the meeting room and sat at a table. I recognized most of the others, since we were all part of the same Detox Program. One of the counsellors read The Twelve Steps Program, and then I listened as a few people introduced themselves. Then it was my turn. I didn't know what to say, so I merely repeated what others had done. It was weird saying, "Hi, my name is Billy and I'm an alcoholic and an addict." I didn't say another word that night.

The words resonated within. For the first time, it occurred to me that maybe that's what I was – an alcoholic and an addict. A quick glance at my resume should have made it clear to anybody who was looking, but I had been specializing in denial, so it never really dawned on me that I had been the one to cause all of the troubles in my life. I thought it was Sharon or maybe Ellen, or Paul (that snake), or Jean. But, that night was the first time I pieced together that if Jean and Billy had a problem, and Ellen and Billy had a problem, and Sharon and Billy had a problem, then maybe the problem was Billy.

It was April 1999, and the earliest I could get into the 28-day program, I was told, was at least a month away. I begged my counsellors to let me into the program. They said they couldn't do anything about it. They said others were waiting. "Rules are rules," they said. "It's full and you just have to come back in a month," they told me. I knew I could never do it; I had nowhere to live and I couldn't stay sober for a month and come back. No way! I was surely going to die! I had just gotten over the worst of it, and I knew I couldn't survive the Detox Centre twice in one lifetime. I was so scared!

Strange as it may seem, I had never stopped my childhood habit of praying every night. Well, maybe not *every* night, but I never forgot that God was there and that I needed his help from time to time. Not that I ever felt like I was in a position to tell God what to do, or that He owed me anything. I'm not sure what happened, but I think the Almighty pulled a few strings for me, because at the end of the week I was told that there had been a cancellation and that I could go into the program I needed so desperately! To this day, I don't really think that was true. I think they saw that I really, sincerely wanted it – that I needed it – and they knew that I knew it, too. I didn't know what to call 'it', but somewhere that week, I began what's called recovery. Someplace between Sudbury and Elliot Lake; somewhere between Spanish and the Centre; sometime between my last beer and my first meeting; a miracle had begun. There I began a life and death struggle with my addictions.

One of the first things I can remember about that place was a big poster with the Twelve Steps written on it. I read them (I had first heard them a few times over in the Detox Centre), but they never sank in the way they did this time. I felt something… a calm of sorts came over me and I thought to myself, maybe there really is a way out of this.

This Centre is a first-class facility, and I would recommend it to anyone. There is a Doctor on staff, and many counsellors who are in recovery themselves. They don't take any crap from anyone. If you don't follow the rules – you're gone. They make you face your fears; if you don't like someone, you can bet they'll make him your roommate or they'll make sure you confront each other over any issues you've had.

The point of rehab is to face up to the unmanageable person you've become. It's not much fun, and at some points it's tough, challenging, and even shocking. But eventually, if you stay with it, you learn a ton about your addiction, your habits, and even yourself; in the end, it's a worthwhile journey. But going through it… well, that's a different story.

There are classes from early morning until late at night. It's all about keeping you busy, keeping you occupied, so you don't have time to languish in self-pity – and retooling your mind so you can start seeing life differently. The counsellors are sharp. They've been on this trek themselves and they know all the scams that addicts can pull, so they are on guard about being played. But when the time is right, and when you've demonstrated you've learned the rules of the game, they can be the biggest help to recovery. Every addict has learned how to make people play by their own rules, but not these counsellors. They hold to a no-nonsense code of good recovery: no manipulation, honest and open interaction and a strong dose of self-discipline.

The day started between 6:00 a.m. and 8:00 a.m. with your morning check-in with the Doc. You'd fall in line and wait for the invariable question, "So how are you?" This was your one opportunity in the day to present any concerns: medical, emotional or otherwise. You could give just about any answer to that question. You could say good or bad or scared, but not fine! In the Centre, we all knew that 'fine' was a cop-out. It meant:

F – freaked out
I – insecure
N – neurotic
E – emotional

I was told that 'fine' is not a feeling, and I was there to deal with my feelings and talk about exactly how I felt!

Then we would head to the dining hall where we made our own breakfast. The possibilities were endless. The fridge was stocked with tons of stuff. The key was that you chose what you wanted, you cooked it and you cleaned it up. For some of us, even that little bit of responsibility was a challenge.

Next item on the agenda was "Small Group" with your counsellor. This is where we built relationships and dealt with the personal part of the program. The "Small Group" session was followed by some sort of large group event, whether it was a lecture or a movie that would challenge us all on issues of substance abuse.

By now, it was lunch time with more work involved: serving, bussing tables or washing dishes. Everyone had a daily duty for each week, and while duties rotated from mopping floors to cleaning hallways, you couldn't get away without fulfilling your responsibilities!

From there, it was back to the classroom to study more about your addiction. Once more, it could be a speaker or small group discussion, a film, or an activity. One thing was clear: participation was mandatory. Think you're too good to get involved? Think again! What's the matter? Nothing to say? You'd better find something. When I first began, I was one of those last people. I hated being pointed out and forced to make a comment. But before the program was through, I actually looked forward to those sessions.

About mid-afternoon, we broke from the heavy-duty stuff. The recreation period was kind of like recess in school. There was volleyball or horseshoes, paths to walk on or just plain hanging out with people. The activity time went on until supper with only one simple rule: you had to stay out of your room. If you wanted to be alone, you could, but you weren't allowed to escape completely or just go to bed and sleep.

After dinner, it was back to group sessions of some kind. As time went on, we might even walk into Elliot Lake to participate in an AA meeting, just to get the hang of it. By about 9:30 p.m., it was mandatory to gather in the Doyle Lounge for snacks, social time and the only hour of TV allowed – usually the news! I met a few women playing euchre, though fraternization was taboo and a lot of people had been kicked out for it. The mantra in recovery programs is that if you see someone you're attracted to, run the other way, because they're probably sicker than you are. I've lived long enough to discover how true that was.

After the Doyle Lounge, it was bedtime (with an understanding that lights were out by 11:00 p.m.). And while I couldn't have any medication to help me, after a day of self-examination and growing self-awareness; a day filled with other people and exploring their problems, I was just plumb tuckered out. I began to sleep better at night for the first time in years – that solid, sound slumber – the kind that restores your soul and soothes your mind. I slept deeply and peacefully… until 6:00 a.m. and then it all began again.

Sunday afternoons were the only time we were allowed to have visitors – and only for a couple of hours. I would watch sadly as some of the others in the program entertained their guests – usually, they were family members. One day, somewhere near the end of my stay at the Centre, I was told that I had a visitor… so I made my way curiously to the Doyle lounge, wondering who it might be. Much to my surprise, there was my old buddy, Brian. Man, it was good to see him. I honestly don't remember anything we talked about, but I showed him around the facilities and we went for a walk on the trails. I don't think I've ever told Brian how much that meant to me. I really appreciated the effort he made to drive three hours to Elliot Lake – just to cheer me up. I was told later when I got home that Bobby and Gordie came up one day during the week, but it wasn't visiting time, so they were refused entry and were asked politely to leave. Knowing there are people from the outside world who care about you – the fact that you're still alive – can really lift your spirits.

Chapter 9:
Embarking on the Twelve-Step Journey

The "Twelve Steps" originate from Alcoholics Anonymous (AA), the grandfather of all recovery programs. They were developed by genuine alcoholics who discovered this was the only way they could get a hold of their lives. Bill Wilson (Bill W.) and his friend, Dr. Bob Smith, found freedom from their personal hells by applying the principles of AA to their own lives and spreading the word to others like them. Over the decades, Alcoholics Anonymous has proved to be an effective method for helping alcoholics and co-dependents find liberty. Part of its success is its simplicity and clarity. AA is not a social club or a church; it's not an organization or an institution; it's just a bunch of addicts getting together to help each other out of their addictions. And the only thing AA does is continually work its way through twelve basic 'steps' which lead to sobriety. The Big Book, which is kind of the Bible at AA, puts it this way: "Rarely have we seen a person fail who has thoroughly followed our path."

What is that path? The first day at the Centre, I probably still hadn't understood that I was about to embark on the journey of a lifetime. It was a roller coaster ride of chills and thrills and spills, but eventually it unravelled the knotted mess of my life and made it manageable and pliable. The Twelve Step path worked for me – but not without a ton of blood, sweat and tears. You'll probably begin to understand why as you look them over.

1. We admitted we were powerless over alcohol; that our lives had become unmanageable.

2. We came to believe that a power greater than ourselves could restore us to sanity.

3. We made a decision to turn our will and our lives over to the care of God as we understood Him.

4. We made a searching and fearless moral inventory of ourselves.

5. We admitted to God, to ourselves, and to another human being the exact nature of our wrongs.

6. We were entirely ready to have God remove all these defects of character.

7. We humbly asked Him to remove our shortcomings.

8. We made a list of all persons we had harmed, and became willing to make amends to them all.

9. We made direct amends to such people wherever possible, except when to do so would injure them or others.

10. We continued to take personal inventory and when we were wrong promptly admitted it.

11. We sought through prayer and meditation to improve our conscious contact with God as we understood Him, praying only for knowledge of His will for us and the power to carry that out.

12.   Having had a spiritual awakening as the result of these steps, we tried to carry this message to alcoholics, and to practice these principles in all our affairs.

They're twelve simple steps, but what a pile of determination, discipline and just plain old guts it took to live them out. It's all about personal ownership: taking responsibility for your life and what you make of it. It's got to do with reshaping an entire lifestyle by changing a series of small habits and re-crafting new habits to take their place, until your whole approach to life has been retooled. In the end, it's about life-change – transforming the impossible until it becomes the implacable. But just how does it happen?

The recovery movement is filled with acrostics and inspirational phrases to keep you focused and encourage you through the journey. One of the first things you learn is the answer to the question, 'HOW'?
> H – Honest
> O – Open
> W – Willing

It all starts there! You've got be honest enough to face yourself, to take a hard look at the realities that have resulted from your choices. Once you've done that, it takes a courageous openness to the possibility of change. That would be a whole lot easier if it didn't come with a lot of correction, and criticism; unless you can take both from others and yourself, you won't get far. Still, it gets disheartening along the path; you want to throw in the towel and go back on your resolve, but just like another AA saying goes… "Don't leave five minutes before the miracle!" That's why the process requires an ongoing willingness that refuses to quit – and even when that gives out – a willingness to be made willing!

You learn very quickly in a 28-day program that nothing happens overnight. You didn't create this mess in a day, and you won't clean it up that quickly either! The classes and assignments were really hard. They were intended to be. They involved hours of deep reflection, and the group sessions weren't any easier. They required ruthless honesty in front of a group of others, who, if they were worth their space at the circle, wouldn't let you off the hook. We were taught to challenge ourselves and others in the group. There was no "easier, softer way," as it says in the Big Book. We had to "feel our feelings and confront our fears" both privately and in front of others.

There wasn't a brain cell or muscle fibre in me that liked or wanted to do any of this. From childhood, I hated school. All that homework, and thinking, and especially when they made you stand in front of the class to recite something or speak publicly. I was much more comfortable in my little cocoon. Remember the Simon and Garfunkel song, "I am a Rock"… "I touch no one and no one touches me… and a rock feels no pain, and an island never cries." That was me.

But they say good recovery comes from the far side of despair, and this was as desperate as I could get. I told myself that I am here for recovery! I'll do whatever it takes! So when they said this is what I had to do to get better, I was determined that I would do it! People don't change until the pain of changing is less than the pain that they're in right now. At first, I worried that I wouldn't get all the assignments done! But eventually, I discovered that I didn't mind doing the homework, after all. I was starting to understand what made me tick, and I liked that. And while I never became the Dale Carnegie of AA, I made the effort, grew a little and actually enjoyed sharing my stuff with the group! It became life-changing for me.

The counsellors gave us all kinds of feedback and there were lots of rules to follow. It definitely wasn't the Hilton. Some of the counsellors' comments were encouraging, but they could be pretty cutting when they had to be. They didn't hold punches, and we all discovered with these folks that the adage is true, "You can't con a con." These guys had heard it all – mostly because they had lived it all themselves! And they were relentless about the rules – everything was done by the book. Skipping class or even being late was a capital offense. Justice was meted out regularly, day or night, in the Doyle Lounge. We'd be called out of a class or rec time by a voice on the PA announcing an immediate Community Meeting. Pretty soon, we all recognized what that meant. Everyone, from every group and every activity, had to drop what they were doing to witness a public trial. Someone was being kicked out of the Centre because of their behaviour. The attitude was: if you weren't serious about working the program, there's the door. They could be the kindest, gentlest people to help you, but once you crossed the line, it was like being exiled… you're gone!

The program lasted four weeks – and was kind of like going to university. I was in the freshman class, and each week got just a little harder and dug a little deeper. Every Friday, a group left, ready to face the world with their new-found sobriety. We would have a celebration for the graduates, complete with speeches, affirmations and congratulations. They all looked so happy, almost glowing! Family and friends were invited, and were encouraged to say a few words. For some guests, it was a tear-filled experience; for others, it raised more of a wait-and-see attitude. They had obviously been through the process before and were maybe wondering if they'd have to do it again.

To me, the farewells were always kind of sad. You share your heart and soul with complete strangers and discover a profound bond between a few new friends, and you do your portion of wondering, too. Will I ever reach that day myself? Will I ever see Frank again? What would it be like if I met Sarah on the street? These were all things I wondered. The truth is, the Centre is like a microwave oven where you bake instant intimacy and relationships that go a mile deep but only a few feet in breadth. They're real and helpful at the time, but they're also temporary and disposable, and probably couldn't stand the light of day. As I said goodbye to those who left us, I knew I probably would never see them again; each parting hug conveyed that sadness, along with the hope that this one or that one would overcome his or her own special obstacles and ultimately make it in the long run.

It was spring in the North. The snow had all but vanished, the ground was soft and the air full with the aroma of new life. On May 14, 1999, I had been sober for one month! It was quite a milestone! I was really changing. I was getting up early; making my bed; showering daily; brushing my teeth; writing in my journal; praying and reading the AA books! I know, I know, that doesn't sound like much – after all, who doesn't brush their teeth or shower? But for me, these were the building blocks of normalcy; the foundations of a regular, functioning life. Even though that tells you how broken my life actually was, the changes really were something to celebrate! Not only did I see a change, but I could feel it, too. It was a growing confidence that compounded each day – like money in the bank. It was the recovery of memories: some as simple as recalling the topic of yesterday's lecture, others as profound as revisiting my Mom's death and finally experiencing the emotion. It meant a deepening clarity about who I was, and beginning to wonder where I was going. I was sleeping and eating regularly, something I hadn't done for years! I gained back some weight and was exercising, mostly through long walks in the forest. Each day that spring felt better than the last.

I learned that when I started using, I had stopped growing emotionally. To really experience recovery, I would have to go back and pick up the loose ends of my life from when I was 17. As I attended lectures and groups, I began to see how I could actually do that. I realized that my peers in high school had been thinking about their futures, planning on education and preparing for careers, all while I was thinking about the next joint and planning for the next party. While others were transitioning from girlfriends to fiancés, I was still trying to figure out how to score with that chick by getting high with her. Some of my stoner buddies had begun to control their drug use; my drug use, on the other hand, was simply controlling me. It took me until now to see the difference between addictive behaviour, and kids just having fun. I was clearly the former; many of my peers at that age were the latter. Somehow they outgrew it – I didn't.

Now, thirty years later (yeah, count 'em... thirty!), I understood something had to change. It was made clear to me that I can't use because I can't quit! I can't drink/use or I'm screwed. I have a physical and mental dependency on these two poisons. If it was in my sight or within my reach, it was an uncontrollable urge to drink or use, and I just couldn't put myself in that position anymore. It was just too dangerous. I could finally see how high the stakes actually were!

I was learning so many things! Whenever I heard someone
say something that made sense to me, I wrote it on the back
page of my journal. It is a list I live by to this day. As I look it
over right now, each hard-won lesson means so much to me
that I can't figure out which ones to share and which ones
will seem trite to others. It's mainly all typical 'AA stuff'…
"Let go and let God", "Easy does it", "One day at a time". But
each of these pithy sayings have proven to be lifelines to me
at one point or another. Here are just a few you might not
have heard before…

- If I put half the effort into sobriety as I did to getting
  drunk and stoned… IT WILL WORK!
- If you compare yourself with others, you will become
  vain or bitter, for always there will be greater and lesser
  persons than yourself.
- I'm being FREED – not being deprived!
- Stay away from the first drink/toke and you'll never get
  drunk/stoned again.
- I did not know what God was like until I lifted a hand to
  help someone else.
- Don't drive forward while continuing to look in your
  rear-view mirror.
- I thought I drank because I had problems; now I see that I
  had problems because I drank.

It was like an awakening. I'd been lost in a fog for so long,
that I thought being dazed and confused was normal. Now
the mists were parting and light was dawning. I saw things
that I had never seen before. Beauty was surrounding me on
every side… where had I been? Everything in my life had
been grey and beige – now there was colour in life – vivid
colour! The plants and trees were… well, they were green!

The sky was blue! The sun was brilliant and even the rain was beautiful! All of these thoughts I charted in my journal, which in the program was handed to your personal counsellor. One day, Ralph replied to one of my letters and said, "The more you wake up, the more you will feel. Express the feelings as they come."

He also wrote: "You will come to understand that nothing should distract you from recovery. It's through good recovery that you deal with life as it comes. Your life is just as important as anyone else's. Your history is yours. You don't need to experience anymore negative consequences due to drinking. Live and have fun!" He was right about good recovery. It's the key to coping with reality.

I was coming to the end of the program. One night, I wrote in my journal, "Two more sleeps and I'm on my way home to take on the outside world. It makes me feel good and sad and scared all at the same time." It was amazing to think I had come this far, but it seemed impossible to imagine I could go a step further. How could I do this without the friends I had made at the Centre? What would I do outside the secure environment of the Centre, shaded from the influences of the outside world? But I went on, in the journal, to take inventory of what was going on here anyway. I knew God was working in my life because:
1. I was at rehab
2. I was working the program
3. I saw things changing (e.g. my personality, confidence and self-worth)
4. I didn't worry as much
5. I could see the beginnings of a future for me now
6. I handled difficult situations differently
7. I had learned to say, "No" (sometimes)

On my last day, I did my fifth step. This is usually considered a major turning point in twelve-step programs. Few people have the guts and internal fortitude to accomplish the fourth step – the one that requires you to take a "searching and fearless moral inventory" of your life. It's easy to be superficial; to just go through the motions, but the healing is in the pain. To do step four properly takes grit, determination, and a whole lot of courage. But you've entered a different universe when you do the fifth step! This step demands that you share your stuff with another person – all of it… even the stuff you can barely admit to yourself.

I did my fifth step with a guy I'd never met before. Maybe that should make it easier, but when you're trying to tell someone the exact nature of your wrongs, it just seems easier to slide over stuff with someone who knows you. He was an old AA vet. This wasn't his first 'fifth' and wouldn't be his last. I talked and talked and unburdened my heart. He sat there stoically and never said a word. At the end of an hour and a half, it had only seemed like ten minutes, but the deed was done, and my heart was free. I couldn't believe it! What a load that had been gathering, and now it was all gone.

The next two steps involve reflection and re-evaluation. If step five is what Christians call confession, step seven is repentance. At the Centre, they recommended going out for a long, solitary walk. On my own, out in the forest, I began to sort through my issues. While I was out there, though, I had a spiritual awakening while talking to God the best way I knew how. I was afraid to leave. Where would I go? And what I was going to do? I had no job; I had nowhere to live and didn't have a dime to my name.

As I walked down a path and cut through the trees for a snowmobile trail, tears were starting to run down my face. The trees were very tall on each side and closed in on me like two high walls. As I turned a corner, something happened that I couldn't have expected in that shaded spot. Suddenly, the bright sun shone through an opening in the trees directly above me. It was as if a huge spotlight from heaven had singled me out! I felt like God, Himself, was looking down on me! It meant something to me for the sun to arrive at that spot, just as I got there. It was so bright that I couldn't see anything else; it blinded me. All in all, I think it was the sign I was looking for – for me and for my life. I felt that God was giving me His blessing and was telling me, "Billy, I know you, and love you, and it's going to be alright!" At that moment, I began to feel what seemed to be waves of peace flow over me and I was no longer afraid of the future – concerned, yes – but not afraid, because I trusted it would be okay.

When I walked into the Centre a month earlier, I was hopeless. But as I sauntered through those tall pines, I walked out of the shadows and onto the pathway of hope. Later that day, I penned these words: "This is the first day of the rest of my life." And it really was!

It was now my last night there, and all but one in my group had made it. We all felt so close to each other, because we really were. We had come to know a lot about each other… our past, our pain and problems, and we had seen the growth that came with some recovery under our belts. It was a great feeling to know what we had accomplished. But, we also knew that we were just one arm's length away from destruction – if we didn't use what we had been taught in the last 28 days.

We had our last small group with our counsellor. Then we went outside and made a bonfire. We were told that if we wanted, we could burn a lot of our projects that we had done – mostly the ones that had a lot of pain associated with them to put some closure on it and leave it all behind. It was amazing the way that the smoke billowed up into the darkness. You could almost see the guilt, remorse, shame, revenge and whatever else was in those pages dissolving.

Each of us had been asked to make a poster called "The Wall", which represented the specific obstacles we had to overcome. I suppose it was my fondness for cars, or maybe it represented my haste to get free, but I symbolized it as a drag race. The cars all bore sponsor decals from all kinds of hang-ups. They had stickers for sex, drugs, resentment, anger, guilt, shame... That poster was a painful piece of my Centre experience, and along with my hand-written fourth step, I gladly burnt both. As the flames rose, my tears flowed. It felt like being unshackled – set free! It was an awesome night and at the end, we all hugged each other as we whooped and hollered! It was one of the most touching moments I have ever had.

The next day at the end of our 28 days, there was a "farewell". We don't call it a "graduation", because we will never "graduate" from being an alcoholic or an addict. I asked my sister, Ardie, to attend. She said yes, provided my older sister could drive her to Elliott Lake. I agreed, although I hadn't spoken to Sharon since she had closed me down, and I have to admit, there was still a lot of resentment there! Again, I will let her tell about that day.

Sharon's Story:

Ardith and I arrived on time to sit with the family members of others saying, "Farewell". We were amazed at how few were there. Every-one in the room, including us, had to introduce him or herself. I was shocked at how many said, "I'm _____ and I'm an alcoholic, or an addict." This included all the instructors! It was one of the most moving experiences that I have ever had. The tears flowed out the whole time.

Each person in the inner circle was spoken to directly. Some of the comments were harsh, but when the head instructor came to Bill, he made a comment that Bill was one of the most caring people there and he felt that Bill would make it.

On our way out, a tiny lady spoke to Ardie and myself. She asked if we were Bill's sisters. When told that we were, she commented on what a fine, caring person Bill was to her. She had "fare welled" a week earlier. After her husband had died, while still nursing at the local hospital, she had become an alcoholic. She told us that the Sun-day before, which was Mother's Day, Bill had given her flowers and accompanied her to church. This thrilled us, as his life had always been about "ME".

Ardith's Story

I had heard from Bill that he had checked into a rehab center in Elliot Lake. I thanked God for answered prayer. Bill asked me to attend his farewell. He had been angry at Sharon for finally selling the garage due to the high debts. He really didn't want Sharon to attend. Sharon and I both attended the ceremony; we were both so proud to see Bill finish the program. We know our parents in heaven were looking down on him and were proud of him – their prayers had been answered. Bill was the only one in his group that had come from a Christian home.

Chapter 10:
After the Treatment Centre

During my time at the Centre, I met Natalie. She was in the Family Program, which is like Al-Anon – a group for people who have been affected by alcoholics or addicts in their lives. It's amazing what happens when you love an addict; whether it's a parent or spouse, or anyone close who's struggling with addiction, chances are you're going to get sucked into the vortex of pain. Not only will you be conned at every turn, but you're going to get hurt emotionally, or even physically; what's crazier still, you'll probably turn around and facilitate the situation – even protecting the person who's bringing such anguish into your life!

Now the counsellors had warned us about this kind of co-dependency. Particularly, they told us to run if you're attracted to anyone you meet at the Centre... RUN, because sick people attract sick people and they must be sick, too, if they are in rehab with you! It made perfect sense. It was good advice. But I couldn't help it. Instinctively, I knew that my situation was different. Her name was Natalie and she was a beautiful woman with long, blonde, ringlet hair, beautiful eyes, and curves where I liked them. She was HOT! And, of course, that made everything all right... but it was that French accent that aroused me from the start.

We were in group together and had noticed each other. One day, she told a friend she thought I was cute... something about my blue eyes. The mutual magnetism worked its magic, and somehow we found each other at the same card table during social time in the Doyle lounge. We soon became friends and began playing cards together every evening. She was married, but it wasn't a happy arrangement, and she wanted out soon. She lived in Sudbury, too, so we made plans to get together when I got back (as she was finished two weeks before I did).

Once I finished the program at the Centre, I returned to Sudbury – the only place I really knew – and stayed at a motel with some money Ardith gave me. It was tough, to say the least – and lonely! My old, partying friends were all over town, so it was hard to avoid them completely. Wherever I went – it seemed – had a story attached to it, so there was pain on every corner.

Actually, that year is somewhat of a blur. I worked part time at my old garage for awhile, and that was particularly hurtful. Most of my former clients had no idea of what had happened to me, but as we chatted, it was awkward to have to refer them to the new owner, Paul, who used to be my assistant. He was a young guy who had done well for himself and needed to show everybody who was boss. It was pretty demeaning at times, but I had to make money to live somehow!

When you first hit the street after the 28-day intensity of rehab, you really need a group to process your experience with, so treatment centres often offer Aftercare programs. I joined one that was provided by a place called Pinehurst, and we met for two hours every Thursday evening to talk about life in a straight world, and our struggles therein. Nightly AA meetings were also a must for survival, and I attended regularly. One of the meetings usually becomes your 'home group', the one you feel some responsibility for. A couple of the guys I went to Aftercare with, Mike and Jamie, and I joined the same 'home group' and that made the commitment a little easier to keep.

But inside, something else was brewing: I was crazy about Natalie and made sure we connected once I was back in town. The fact that she was married never stopped me. We got together for coffee a few times after meetings, and the connection grew. She felt sorry for me and wanted to "rescue" me. I enjoyed being felt sorry for, and liked the idea of being rescued, so it seemed like a match made in heaven. We talked about my living situation, and Natalie came up with a creative idea; she and her husband owned an apartment building and needed a handyman – if I was willing to do the occasional odd job, I could live there for free! One of the fringe benefits was that Natalie would come by occasionally to make sure things were copasetic. Those visits became a high point in my newly, non-high life, and, of course, one thing led to another and we fell in love – or was it just lust?

Anyway, things were great until Natalie's husband, Ron, started showing up to check on the building, too. Ron had no clue about what was going on with Natalie and I. She was a rescuer, and as far as he was concerned, I was just another one of her strays. Besides, what could she possibly see in me: a broken, down-on-his-luck addict, when her husband was practically a millionaire and drove a brand new Harley? He had all the toys a guy could possibly want, plus a smokin' hot wife. And me? I didn't have a pot to pee in. But the more he showed up, the more guilty I felt. It's not that he ever came close to catching us – just that I knew deep down – I was doing something wrong. Really wrong!

Things between Ron and Natalie had been tense for awhile, and his issues were part of what brought Natalie to the

Centre in the first place. But Natalie's obsession with me wasn't helping things, and though she never told him about it, eventually, they decided on a separation after fifteen years of marriage. Needing a place to live, Ron moved into the same building I was in. All of a sudden, my little get-togethers with Natalie became a huge problem. I had to move again!

The only place I had to live now was at my old friend Ernie's apartment. I had a bed, but no closet because it was being used for a grow-op. After a short while, I started to drive a taxi. I needed to sleep during part of the day, as I drove nights, but it was almost impossible! The drugs were there in abundance and so was the temptation! Every day the Drop-In Centre began about 9:30 a.m. Ernie and his buddies would sit around all morning, drinking coffee and getting high. The aroma of weed filling the apartment became too much. I knew I had to find another place so that I wouldn't relapse!

Natalie had the answer. She got me a place to live at her best friend's house that was on a lake, just outside of town. It was a pretty swanky spot with a granny flat, which was built for her Dad who had recently died. I moved into the apartment and enjoyed the surroundings: the lakeside view, the feeling of being out in the country and the crystal water that invited me in for a dip at the end of a shift in the cab… it was rich! And to top it off, more often than not, Natalie would be waiting for me in bed when I got home.

I was still pretty foggy in the head – even after four months of sobriety – but driving a cab was something I could handle for the time being. The job was okay, but the money was only good on weekends. So I started driving 3:00 p.m. until 3:00 a.m. over the weekend and two other days in the week. One of my worst memories while driving cab happened just before Christmas that year: I got a call to pick up Ernie and some friends. I arrived at the address and out came a few couples. All of the guys used to work for me at the shop. They were headed to the new owner's Christmas party. It was very embarrassing letting them off at the Christmas party that I hosted a year earlier. Now I was just some schmuck driving hack, taking them on their big night out. I sat for a minute and looked inside as I fought back the tears. Talk about a humbling moment!

Through the winter months, I managed to keep my plowing truck on the road, too. Although I cut down on my contracts, it was tough to swing both jobs. Some nights I'd drive cab until 3:00 a.m., then go plowing until around noon before I could sleep for a couple hours, and then I'd hop back in the cab. During some of those Northern Ontario storms, I'd do the same drill for two or three nights in a row and get completely exhausted. But, somehow, I managed to stay clean and still work my program.

I spent my days off with Natalie. I suppose it was love... of a kind... but neither of us had experienced enough healing to make for a healthy whole. Still, in spite of the dysfunction that permeated the relationship, God used Natalie to inspire a clear vision of recovery in my life. She had been here before. Ron had been in AA for a long time and Natalie had her "Black Belt" in Al-Anon and was a fixture there – the program for the loved ones of alcoholics. She knew how to hold me to account on the program: wouldn't put up with any bull, and walked through some of the toughest parts of my recovery with me. Natalie knew that family was important. She was the one who encouraged me to patch things up with Sharon and Ken, and she drove over to Manitoulin Island with me for our first real reunion since the Centre.

Natalie and I spent the next year together. I never lived with her, but we saw each other as much as possible and we dreamed of being married someday. Still, there was no escaping the essential dysfunction of our relationship. The co-dependency we had established had doomed it from the start. I had made her my drug of choice – something I was told in treatment not to do. Now I had to pay the price. Just before my first birthday, (the celebration of my first year of sobriety), she went back to her husband. It was very painful for me. She was all I knew now; my only support system. Somehow, though, with a lot of prayer and my buddies, Jamie and Mike from the Aftercare Group, I managed to get through that season without drinking or drugs. Jamie and Mike would listen for hours on end as I lamented my lot, listening over and over again to my tale of woe, and loving me through it all. I finally had to accept that this was God's best for us. I had prayed and asked the Lord to guide my life as He saw fit, and this seemed to be His answer. I had to rely on Him. What else could I do?

Chapter 11:
Facing the Root Issues

The Bible says, "Whatever your hand finds to do, do it with all your might." And that's what I tried to do. Natalie was gone, the lake house was gone, and all there was left for me at this point was the cab. I was still driving taxi and trying to get through each shift. My heart was heavy, and though I hadn't yet become a committed Christ-follower, I thought of myself as being pretty 'spiritual' now. I guess I was seeking. I prayed and prayed, and journaled and journaled. And then I'd pray again. Driving cab is a lot like life... you never know where the next fare will take you, and you never know who you will meet. But that's another book in itself.

I was working late nights, and the bars were where you made money. I spent many a lonely night, just sitting there, watching the traffic going in and out of the bars: groups of guys who were out for a good time, couples who were snuggled together against the cold, derelicts too, and people at various points along their downward spiral. Many of my pick-ups were old drinking buddies. At first, they would make comments like, "Oh, you won't last long. You'll soon be back drinking with us." Everybody, it seemed, had a friend-of-a-friend story about someone who had gotten it together, only to fall back into the sewer. These stories were always peopled by addicts just like me, who couldn't come to terms with their addictions. But, at the same time, like me again, they knew something was wrong. But none of my buddies could actually believe that I would escape the trap for good. And to be honest, I still wasn't so sure myself. Many of them were addicts, too, and couldn't stop the destructive cycle of addiction. Most of them couldn't even see it.

I had lots of time to think about their questions and, eventually, the answer came to me: I KNEW BETTER! I had come from a Christian home. I had loving parents, and sisters who were concerned about me and I had people praying for me. Most of my friends were just doing what life had programmed them for. They had seen it in their families all their lives! Drunken dads who might not come home for a few days at a time, or even worse, who might come home and take it out on their wives and kids – like I did occasionally.

Eventually, I figured out that I couldn't just go to the bar with my buddies, have a pop and shoot a game of pool. It wasn't safe. I didn't feel comfortable; I didn't belong there anymore, but my friends were there. That's when some of the Centre training kicked in. I had to stay away from those "people, places and things if I want to stay sober," AND always have a backup plan. For instance, when the boys suggested that we hang out for the night, I needed some healthy friends I could turn to. "Sorry," I'd say, "I've got to meet somebody tonight." Even so, there were hard days – especially now without Natalie – I felt lost!

I was hanging out with Mike and Jamie a lot, and Jamie invited me to church one day. He'd been going to the Salvation Army church for about a year, so I went. It was a smaller church than the one I had gone to, and the people were mostly older, but they were friendly and kind. They sang songs I remembered from my childhood, and it started to feel like home.

One of the men playing in the Band looked familiar. As soon as the service was over, he came down to see me. He said,

"Bill Moore?" and when I said that I was, he told me this story: his name was Wilson and he used to come to the garage. Since both he and my Dad were Christians, over the years, they had become friends. Apparently, my Dad had shared his concern over my lifestyle and asked Wilson to pray for me. That day at church, he told me that he had prayed for me for years. He was so excited that he could hardly contain his joy seeing me in church.

Still, even with the church connection, I was struggling with some pretty profound pain that wouldn't go away – no matter what I did. I missed Natalie so much and I wasn't sure if I was going to slip and drink or use drugs again! It didn't help that, every once in awhile, I'd see her speeding by on the back of a Harley; her blonde curls flowing out of the back of her helmet, her arms around Ron and not me. It came to me that I needed to get help to deal with this loneliness inside of me. I knew that the Centre that I attended last year, had a two – week Relapse Prevention Program. They had recommended it for people who had made it through the 28-day program, usually one to three years later. It occurred to me now, about a year out of the Centre, that maybe that's what I needed. I made the call to see if I could get into the program, and a few weeks later I went.

It felt so good walking in the doors of that place. I didn't know anyone in my group, but it felt like home. We all made friends fast in the group, and it was great. I had now been clean and sober for twelve months. It was good to look at the big picture and remember where I was only a year ago! But – on the other hand – I was so close to falling off the wagon. Losing Natalie had been a terrible shock and I needed more tools to survive. I remembered what happened to me with Ellen. I couldn't let that happen this time! I held on to God and prayed some more. I desperately wanted to stay on the path God had chosen for me.

It was good to get back and learn more about my disease. Some of things I was taught this time were: that it is a disease of lying and deceit. One usage will trigger a cycle of craving. There is no such thing as a slip. I would need extended care for two years. Relapse is not uncommon; only a third of the people who go through a program stay sober after the first time in rehab; another third relapse within three to five years and the last third relapse regularly for the rest of their lives.

What is relapse? Most people think that it is going back to alcohol and drug use. That's the old theory. Now, we know that alcohol and drug use are the last result of relapse. Just as recovery begins in the mind, relapse begins there, too. There are all kinds of triggers, and they gave us some handy acrostics to remember them.

For instance HALT leads to relapse:

    H – hungry
    A – angry
    L – lonely
    T – tired

So often, our emotional responses to situations set in motion a series of reactions that can cascade out of control. The knee-jerk reflex is to turn to your drug of choice. Too happy, too sad – both can be danger zones for the addict. The trick is to learn how to remove the crests from waves and troughs of life, and live in the golden mean. Avoiding intense reactions or extreme moods prevents the domino run that ends in abuse. It's all about taking situations as they come, and remembering as the Ancient King said, that "this, too, shall pass." That's what it means to live life on life's terms.

Maybe the biggest button is PLOM:

P – poor
L – little
O – old
M – me

Feeling sorry for yourself is a sure-fire way of whisking the carpet from under your feet and finding yourself in that downward spiral to the bottle. It's so easy to write each story in your life as a tragedy in which you are the miserable victim, unjustly put upon by family and friends, circumstances and situations, and ultimately God Himself. It's a scenario in which you can never win, and one in which you will never find anyone to commiserate with you. So back you go, to the bottle, or the needle, or whatever dysfunctional behaviour brings you solace.

As I was beginning to part the mists of confusion, I wrote in my journal these six warning signs of relapse… triggers to which I was most susceptible:

Denial
Depression
Self pity
Forgetting gratitude
Immature wishes to be happy
Irregular sleep

I was continuing to work on my recovery – especially my focus. I needed to get my mind off Natalie, instead of replaying every scenario, every word she ever spoke to me as though my entire future hung on the thread of her whim. I was finally finding myself – bit by bit. Each person there added a small piece to the puzzle of my life and recovery. There were definite signs of improvement in my head and in my heart. The pain was starting to subside, and I was getting off the Natalie treadmill once in awhile and realizing how good life was – with her or without her. Eventually I came to the breaking point: I was realizing that I had to let go of Natalie. I had to cut that thread that kept me hanging if I was to survive. It just seemed like a six-inch cable though, in the cutting.

My counsellor suggested that I write her a letter to say goodbye, and that I read it to all my peers. It seemed like such good idea as he offered it, but that letter proved a killer to write. It must have taken me a couple of days to actually compose it; it was full of anger and tears, betrayal and regret. Then came the day I had to read it out loud. All of a sudden, it didn't seem like such a great idea after all. How did I get into this mess? But I sat there and squirmed. Man, it was hard. I started crying and could hardly make it through – but one whining sniffle at a time – I did. And when it was over, I felt so much better.

I had prayed so much to God to relieve me of the pain I had in my heart, and now He had begun the healing. I decided to totally turn my will and life over to Him again. I made putting God in the driver's seat a priority as I left the Centre at the end of two weeks. This time, saying goodbye wasn't so hard. I had discovered that a "normal" whole person has body, mind and spirit at the core, but an addict has body, mind and SELF at the core. I was determined to get rid of SELF and develop the spirit.

I also learned that the total recovery process is slow. The first three years are rapid and account for 75% of the recovery.

From three to nine years the recovery continues, but now it's a discipline. The newness and freshness of new life have dimmed, and you get down to the everyday business of living life on life's terms. Some say total recovery takes from 9 to 10 years. Personally, I don't think you ever totally RECOVER! I think it's an ongoing process of renewing your dedication to the principles that set you free in the first place.

One of the movies we watched in the Relapse Prevention Program was "The Elephant in the Room". It was about this family that had an elephant right in the middle of their living room. It just stood there – as big as life – but the family was used to it. They went about their business as if it wasn't even there. They walked around it, went under it, anything just to avoid admitting that it existed. A lot of families have some major issues that stare them right in the face daily, but they simply ignore them, avoid them, and do everything they can not to talk about them. In the recovery world we have a word for that: it's called denial – and as famous writer Mark Twain put it, it's not a river in Africa. It was something I had become a pro at, and now it had to stop. I realized that I needed to deal with things in my path and not ignore them.

As I left the Centre for the last time, I wrote a prayer to capture that commitment:

GOD, I thank You for being a kind, loving God, and that You've seen fit to let this whole series of crises, and the reality of recovery happen in my life. I don't know where it will end up. I am just very thankful it has come to a head now. I know You will be with me--to guide and watch over me--to make new footprints on my new path. God, thank You so much for everything that You've put on my path. I will use each thing, good and bad, as a learning experience. Amen.

Chapter 12:
A Fresh Start

Having left the Centre the second time, with a whole new outlook and a few days of vacation left, I went down to Burlington to visit my sister and her family. Ardie was always great to talk to. She had an innate understanding of me and my journey. I'm sure she wondered if I was out of the woods and how long it might be before I fell apart again Throughout our visit, she invited me to move to Burlington and get a job there. One day, as we were driving somewhere, I talked about driving a taxi and how much I hated it. She asked one more time, why I couldn't move from Sudbury and get a job in Southern Ontario. Just then, a cab pulled up beside us at a light, and as I looked across, I got a sick feeling just glancing at the yellow door with the checkerboard. All the emotions of that lonely prison (which I called a cab back home) welled up within me – and I decided there and then – there was absolutely nothing holding me in Sudbury, and all kinds of possibilities were beckoning me South.

Burlington, though, didn't hold any attraction to me. But Ardie had a daughter, Tracey, who used to be a drinking buddy of mine and she was living in Cambridge. I thought I'd visit her for a couple of days. Tracey's job involved helping people find work, so she helped me with my resume. I sent it out to a bunch of different places, none of which were automotive – I didn't feel like my head was straight enough to work on cars.

The very next day I had a job in construction – something I had never done before. It was interesting how it came about. I went for an interview. The owner asked why, at 48, was I looking for a manual job at base pay. I told him I was a recovering alcoholic and addict and that I had lost everything, and was starting over (something I later learned not to say to everyone I met). On the spot, I was hired! It turned out Ed was a Christian, and instead of rejecting me because of my past, he said I was one of the few honest people he had interviewed and he sensed I needed a chance.

So I hightailed it back to Sudbury, got some stuff, and brought it down to Cambridge and moved in with my niece, Tracey. She was unbelievably hospitable and kind. She took me to Home Depot and bought me all the tools I would need on the new job, trusting me to pay her back on my first pay cheque. We shared the grocery bill and Tracey cooked dinner every night. I paid a little rent, and I slowly got my feet on the ground.

The work was tough! I had done nothing manual in two years, and now I was doing heavy-duty work every day. Monday was hard; Tuesday was harder; by Wednesday I could hardly move, because my muscles were so sore. But come Friday, I was doing better! After three weeks, though, I decided this wasn't the career for me. Digging trenches, carrying around hundred-pound forms and setting them up to pour concrete, then stripping it down to do all over again was more than I could take. It was back-breaking and monotonous, and as much as I appreciated Ed's generosity, I had to tell him the truth. I was a licensed mechanic with better than a year's sobriety under my belt, and surely I could find something in my own field. One day, work had slowed a bit and Ed sent me home. I went to a muffler and brake shop and applied for a job – something I was much more familiar with and believed I was finally physically and mentally ready to handle. I was hired, and when I told Ed I was moving on, he was genuinely pleased for me.

All went well for awhile. I was working at the muffler and brake shop, living with Tracey and getting established. Then it happened! I got a call from Natalie. She missed me very much, she said. She loved me, she said, and couldn't stay with Ron any longer. Of course, everything I had just worked so hard to leave behind, was now staring me in the face. What would I do in the moment of truth? Where could I turn?

I caved, of course. She came down for the weekend. Then I went to Sudbury for the weekend and then we started trading, back and forth. It was looking like we were a couple again. This time she was determined to leave her deadbeat husband for good. She was going to move to Cambridge and bring her daughter, but...

Of course there's a but! I already knew, deep down, this wasn't a healthy relationship for me. But even when I struggled in the Centre, even when I wrote the Farewell Letter, I was hoping everyone around me was wrong. It was 'fake it until you make it.' I'd gone through the motions of letting Natalie go, but they didn't know her like I knew her. I knew she'd come back some day. Like the Spinners used to sing:

> *There's always a chance*
> *A tiny spark remains, yeah*
> *And sparks turn into flames*
> *And love can burn once again...*

And here we were! A happy couple again... just the way it was supposed to be, right? All she had to do was break the news to her husband, and it was on. She'd be in Cambridge with me and he'd be stuck in Rock City with the Southern Ontario blues again.

So… the story unfolds. One fateful night, in October, she told him, and he blew a gasket. He stormed out of the house and onto his Harley and sped away like some cheesy B movie. She called me to tell me the news that all systems were a go. But that night, Ron was in a terrible motorcycle accident. The very next day Natalie called to inform me of the news, and all of a sudden our plans were on hold.

We did the commuting thing while Ron was in intensive care, but he wanted her by his side – and dutifully – she went. By the time he was transferred to a room a few weeks later, Natalie had made her decision. She had tried to leave him but she took the accident as a sign that she had to stay.

It turned out I didn't know her or myself as well as I thought I did. The Centre group was right; it had to end. They could see the dysfunction that I had remained blind to. I was very upset. I tried to believe that it was God's will, but I still didn't understand. He took her away, and then brought her back and then took her away again… just as I was getting over her.

What I couldn't see then was the co-dependent nature of the relationship. I still thought I needed her to make me happy. She was my drug of choice, and I imagined that if I had her, everything would be okay. But she was a married woman, with a life in Sudbury and three teenagers. She may have been in an unhealthy relationship herself, but she was in counselling, and every time I tried to contact her, she refused to reply. I waited a long while for her to come back a third time, but she never did. As I understand it, Natalie and Ron have worked things out and are still together today.

If I had to be honest, I still really care about Natalie, even now. She played such an important role in my life during a critical point in time, but I've come a far enough distance to know that my life today would have turned out completely differently if she were in it. I needed to grow as a person and mature, and that couldn't happen in a relationship. There are some things you've got to do in life, all by yourself, and this was one of them. Most of all, there were experiences I still needed to have that may never have happened if I was still addicted to the emotions that our relationship brought.

Striking Out on My Own

As the Natalie thing came to a head, my niece, Tracey, decided to move on in her life. That meant moving in with her boyfriend – and they probably hadn't counted on me joining them! I had to find another place to live. At the same time, my ex-wife, Jean, for financial reasons, decided that my plowing truck should be in her hands. Since it was in her name anyway, she just took it, and there was not a thing I could do about it. Now I was both carless and homeless.

My sister, Ardie, loaned me their old Cressida for awhile. At least I could look for a place to live in style! The car also kept me working, which was essential to finding an accommodation. I looked and looked for a place in Cambridge... but it had to fit my price range. Every night after work, I'd go see a couple of places, but there was nothing. If I liked it, I couldn't afford it, and if I could afford it, I didn't like it; and if it passed those two criteria, there was a waiting list a mile long. Time was getting short, and I was getting uncomfortable. Finally, I answered an ad for a two-bedroom apartment and went on one more wild goose chase. It's easy to wonder whether God is on vacation when we're in these critical situations; easy to imagine that we pray and pray, but somehow we're on hold in heaven. Where is God when you need Him anyway?

I went to check out the listing, and when I got there, I met the owner. This is how God works... It turned out it was my friend, Ed, the same man who had hired me in construction because I was honest and he wanted to give me a chance. He had other people that wanted the apartment, too, but he gave me another chance. I took it and lived there for five years. Ed was a good friend to me and we had some really profound conversations about God, and what He has done to show us his love.

My sister, Ardie, got me some used furniture and Tracey gave me her old dishes, and utensils, and stuff. My buddy, Brian, lent me his truck and Ernie, my Sudbury roomie drove it down with any treasures that I had left behind in the North. These included my faithful bar table (which I have to this day), my smelly goalie equipment and the three masks covering my entire career, which still have a place of honour in my rec room. Still, my living room remained completely empty. It was a year or so before I had anything to put in it. I made my spare bedroom into a den, with an old TV and on old couch. It was a far cry from what I had owned just a few years earlier, but surprisingly enough, I was content! It was home.

Around the same time, I saw an old car on the side of the road with a "For Sale" sign on it. It was a 1986 Pontiac Bonneville – your grandma's grocery-getter, a four-door, plain-jane, six-cylinder automobile... Nothing to it, but it was all I could afford. So I paid five hundred bucks for it and drove it home. That was my 'ride' for the next four years. A little later, I'll tell you about its final destiny.

At the Centre, the rules about fraternization were pretty strictly enforced, but I had still managed to develop an interest in Natalie there that came to haunt me in my after-life. There was another woman at the Centre I grew close to. Her name was Carol. She was in the same group as Natalie and I got to know her pretty well, since she and Natalie had become friends. She didn't drink or drug either. Like Natalie, it was all Al-Anon stuff that brought her there. Carol was very serious about working her program, and that meant something to me.

Because Carol lived in Brampton, when I came to Southern Ontario, I got in touch with her. When Natalie and I were together, Carol was friends with both of us. When Natalie finally decided she was staying with Ron, she even suggested that Carol and I get together. So we began hanging out most weekends. We became fast friends as I could talk with her about Natalie and still have a "date" for weddings, the movies or whatever. I thanked God for her as a friend and as a support. She always cheered me up. While I was romantically drawn to Carol, the feelings weren't mutual, and we still managed to have what seems, in retrospect, a pretty healthy relationship. We both still had our issues to deal with, but we genuinely helped each other along some pretty lonely and painful roads.

It was the fall of 2000 and life was good. I was finally settled in a home, a job, and a spiffy set of wheels. My social life consisted of AA meetings, going to work and watching the New York Islanders and NASCAR on cable. I didn't have what I wanted, but I did have what I needed! I was in close touch with both my sisters. Now it was time to rebuild my relationship with my son.

I knew this would be difficult. Before the train wreck with Crossing Alignment and Jean, things had been fair to midland between us; since the Centre, we'd only had a few encounters, and they hadn't been good ones. Now it had been about a year since we had talked, and I didn't know what to expect. Would he hate me because of the incredible mess I had made of things? Or would he be a little more forgiving because I was putting my life together? After losing the business, I was sure I was nothing but an embarrassment to him. But just maybe he could take a little pride in watching the old man pick himself up. It was a toss-up, but I had to take the risk.

Tyler was now an adult, living in Toronto. He was doing well, managing a funky storefront on upper-crust Queen Street. He had his own life… and it didn't include me. So how would I break in? I thought about it long and hard, and started by phoning him. It was a little awkward, but he didn't hang-up. Eventually, we decided to meet for lunch downtown. Over time, I tried to make amends for all that had gone wrong, but he shut me down. Tyler seemed to be saying that we could have a relationship, but we didn't need to relive the past to do it.

Someone told me in the Centre that relationships are like bank accounts: sometimes you're way overdrawn, and it may take awhile before you've made enough deposits to make another withdrawal. So that's what I'm doing with Tyler: making little love deposits whenever I can and hoping, someday, to have a positive balance in the account. So I keep calling him and we keep talking. At first it was sporadic, but we're up to once a week now. And I drive to Toronto and take him out for dinner, as often as our schedules allow. He has let me into a part of his life, and I'm grateful. But I realize that

I killed all the love there was with my former lifestyle, and restoring that love may take awhile.

He has grown up to be a very independent person – something I'm just getting to be myself. Over the years since reconnecting, from 2000 until now, he's seen some of his dreams become reality, and has his own shop, and is developing a name for himself in business. I am very proud of him.

During this time in my new life, I attended AA meetings as often as I could, and worked the AA plan daily. I was about 1 1/2 years sober by now and seeing an addiction counsellor named Hailey at an addiction counselling facility once a week. She was especially kind and patient. She seemed to know just how to get me to give my best. I could talk to her about anything, and a few times I told her things I'd never told another soul. It helped a lot.

As expected, I was growing rapidly in some areas of my recovery, and more slowly in others. I worked hard on my co-dependency issues with women and relationships. It was pretty obvious: if Jean and Billy have a problem, Ellen and Billy have a problem, and Natalie and Billy have a problem, then Billy must be the problem! Something was desperately wrong with how I related to women. To this day, I'm not sure if I've got it all figured out, but I think I'm doing better.

I went without a meaningful relationship for five years. I think one reason was because I wasn't that sick anymore, so I didn't attract sick women; but I still wasn't healthy enough, so I didn't attract healthy women, either. The bottom line was this: I simply wasn't attracting any women. That's when I recognized that I finally had to learn to love myself, and take care of myself.

I found the insight I needed in a book called The Twelve Steps of Co-Dependency by Melody Beattie. I realized that I had been addicted to relationships and that I am very co-dependent. I had been in a relationship ever since I was 17! I went from my Mom and my two sisters' love, to other women, just to find the love that I had when I was young. I would find some part of that love in every woman I was with throughout the years.

It was very difficult being on my own – without the love of a woman – healthy or otherwise. For the very first time in my life, I had to learn to cook, clean (I'm still not too great at that!), take care of my finances, and all the other stuff that normal people do every day. I had never done any of these things for myself before. But like everything else in my life, I was starting to learn.

Hailey got me involved with another Aftercare program in Kitchener to help me get stronger. It was held every Thursday night at the hospital for 32 weeks. Hailey and another counsellor named Beth became the catalysts for this season of transformation. The sessions consisted of discussions about how our week had gone, a topic for exploration, and then some more talk about life in general – but without our drug of choice. Nothing too fancy, but somehow it was like a lifesaver thrown out to drowning people. Eight of us met regularly and became friends, and then grew into a family. We didn't just go to group; we hung out, were there for each other, and we had a great straight time! I so much looked forward to that group, that I went straight from work to get there early and have a few moments to chat with Hailey. When the group ended, we had to learn to say goodbye, and to move on. The goal was not to become too dependent on anything or anyone.

I was doing pretty good, spending time with Carol on weekends, working on weekdays and going to meetings every night. I thought it was time to 'give back' to society, so I volunteered at a shelter for street kids in Kitchener called ROOF (an acronym for Reaching Our Outdoor Friends). It was my first real experience helping others. I thought I could make a difference as a kind of cautionary tale: you know, "Look at me... you don't want to end up the way I did..." But it wasn't that easy. I discovered that even kids from good homes knew how to play the system... They were out for freebies, food, shelter, and hooking up instead of help. And besides, I was the only volunteer on Staff. Everyone else was being paid, or working on their resume for some school credit. I felt useless, and although I tried to connect with kids, it just wasn't happening. So considering that it made for a very long day (I went there right from work and stayed until 11:00 p.m.), after a couple of months, I decided to give it up. I felt like I was failing again, letting the folks at ROOF down, but I just couldn't feel good about working there.

But, I was now getting bored again. It still seemed hard to pass the time without my toke or a bottle. I could handle sitting around and doing nothing when I was high, but sober – that just didn't work! It was also the first time in my life that I wasn't in a relationship. I was going through a lot of emotional confusion in this sober life, and although my sisters were only a phone call away, I seemed all alone. And even though my addictions seemed at bay, I was feeling confused and sorry for myself. One day I wrote this...

I was a somebody.
Now I'm a nobody!
I knew a lot of people.
I don't know anybody here!

A lot of people liked me.
A lot of people liked me to be around.
I was popular.
I was a businessman with money and new cars and lots of toys.
Believe it or not, I was probably stronger in many ways then.
I had confidence because I had all of THAT!

Nobody knows me here.
I have no history here.

I was a good goalie in hockey.
I was a good mechanic.
I was good at racing.
I was good with women and I don't mean bar girls.

I was! I was! I was!

I only had a bad couple of years and it all changed!

Sometimes that kind of "stinking thinking" can still get
a hold of me. I start to feel sorry for myself – unloved and
uncared for. The loneliness starts to give me a kind of chok-
ing feeling. I've learned no good can come from this state
of mind. I must resist it at all costs. But that doesn't mean it
doesn't creep up on me from time to time.

Life – as I knew it – was shaping up a little differently than I
had imagined. Maybe I thought I could keep being the player,
just without drugs or alcohol. But this new life was starting
to look a lot lonelier: no more parties, no women to impress,
and no money to impress them with. Sobriety was a much
better world to live in, but truth be told, it felt like I lost my
game in the bargain. I had no real desire to go back there, I
just needed to figure out how to survive here! I needed some

kind of healthy way to spend my time. [Enter my old racing buddy, Jeff.]

One day, out of the blue, Jeff called. He was coming South for a wedding, and offered to bring my race truck down from Sudbury. I had almost forgotten about the old '86 Chevy S10 4X4. Back when I was driving it in races a few years earlier, it ran like a top, but after a few Northern winters in the elements, that 454 engine was pretty beat up. I had tried to sell it and even give it away, but no one wanted it. It had been sitting around gathering rust until Jeff called. It wasn't much, but I thought with a bit of work (okay, lots of work!) I could bring it back to life. So Jeff dumped it at my place, and I was off!

Now, to be honest, there's nothing I'd like better right here than to tell you every detail about the miraculous restoration of UFO 454, but I know that would be more for my benefit than yours. So I'll spare you, except to say that it was a piece-by-piece process that took a whole year and over $3,000 – not much considering the amount of work that went into it, but a small fortune considering I was living on fourteen bucks an hour! I knew that the truck could be an unhealthy project for me if I let it consume me, so I laid out a carefully devised work-plan and stuck to it, a little at a time, showing that I actually did learn some stuff from all those programs!

The great discovery took awhile before I could put it together. As I began to spend delightful hours working on the racing truck, mostly in my driveway, it slowly dawned on me: there were things from my past life that could be redeemed. Not everything back there was evil, dark, or dangerous. But I had to have boundaries to make it healthy in the new world I was creating for myself. Within those wise limits around the obsession factor, it was possible to derive great enjoyment from tinkering with a truck and racing it. And that's what I did; filling some of the necessary loneliness of starting a new life with something constructive.

Chapter 13:
Calvary

Life in Cambridge was beginning to feel normal. I had my
own home and a routine that I was starting to enjoy. I was
beginning to feel at home, but I needed something more. The
love and support of a community of people to share life with
was missing, and I didn't know how or when I would find
that. AA was great as far as it went, but it just didn't go far
enough.

As I travelled to work each day, I passed a Pentecostal church
on the main drag. It was like the Cambridge equivalent of
the church I had grown up in. I couldn't help but notice it
every time I drove by, but I put it out of my mind as quickly
as I could. Way too many memories there! Feelings of guilt
and remorse – oughts and ought nots – a huge pile of 'should'
crowded my mind whenever I passed that place. And yet...
there was something there calling me, beckoning me and
drawing me in. All the memories weren't bad ones. There
were images of my parents and their friends, and the joy they
had at Camp Meeting time, melodies of hymns that brought
warmth and nostalgia, and somewhere beyond the rules and
regulations, there was God. And, it turned out (through the
recovery process) that He wasn't so bad.

I had been glad to renew a kind of acquaintance with my
higher power. I enjoyed Him as just that: a 'higher power'.
I wasn't sure I wanted a first-name basis relationship with
Him. We had found a kind of uneasy settlement. Did I really
want to go any farther with Him? Why upset the applecart?

I knew I could find Him in that church, but I could find Him in lots of other places as well. My sister, Ardie, had turned away from Pentecostal stuff and found peace in the Anglican Church. If it worked for her, it could work for me too!

One day, Sharon and I were talking on the phone about churches. She was eager to help me find one. She felt that it would solidify my new path in life, and I kind of agreed. She mentioned Calvary Pentecostal Assembly on Hespeler Road, and I immediately recognized it as the name from the sign in front of that church that I drove by daily. She said that I should check it out, especially because I knew the pastor, David Courey. I couldn't remember at first, then she told me that he was the guy who did Dad's funeral in Sudbury.

All of a sudden, I did remember that pain in the butt. He was good friends with my Dad. He also had his auto repairs done at my Dad's shop where I worked. Every time he dropped his car off, my Dad would insist that I drive him back to the church or home! I know now that he hoped that David would talk to me about spiritual things. I used to hate that ride with him – he was so happy and talkative. I couldn't wait to let him out of the car so I could have some peace and quiet.

Truth is, the guy couldn't win. I knew about pastors! If he tried to give me that gospel stuff, he was a jerk. If he just tried to be nice, he was a jerk. In fact, if he just sat there and shut up (which he never did) he was a jerk. It was torture for me, sheer torture to drive him. He was my sworn enemy. And now my sister was telling me who the pastor was there. That sealed it for me. I definitely wouldn't be visiting that place! Famous last words...

When I was actively helping at ROOF, they suggested that I take a course in Suicide Prevention so that I could help teens on the edge if I needed to. It struck me as a good idea, and I could probably learn some helpful stuff for myself along the way. So I committed to do it, took the information, and, sure enough, it was being held at a church in Cambridge called Calvary. To be honest, I thought twice about going, but I had promised... so I went.

I had thought about how I would feel walking into a Pentecostal church. Would I be angry? Would I feel guilt? Would I be overwhelmed with memories of my parents? But when I got there, the good news was that I didn't have to go into the front door, or walk through the sanctuary. The entrance was in a side door, and the entire two-day session was held in a long narrow room in the basement. But still, I have to admit, I felt something walking into Calvary Pentecostal Assembly. Nothing negative, but a calm, secure warmth. A nice, safe feeling permeated my heart. I was aware of it, but I had no words to explain it.

There were about twenty-five participants, all of them professionals – and there was me – a volunteer (and a reluctant one at that). I was feeling pretty inadequate until I met a remarkably nice woman named Sandy. She began the conversation and kept it going. We talked about everything from why I was there to where I came from. As we chatted, she commented that she had been in Sudbury at the Pentecostal church the week before (at a conference). I told her that I had attended that church as a child. She seemed delighted, and proceeded to recount the details of her trip there. She told me that she had stayed in a wonderful older lady's home. Her name was Ida Nelder. I was mind-boggled! Ida had been my Mother's close friend over the years! They had been prayer partners, and shared each other's burdens. I'm pretty sure they spent plenty of time praying for me, and Mrs. Nelder's son, Gordy. Both of us were playing the part of the prodigal. I began to wonder if God had engineered this moment. It seemed too unlikely to be coincidence. Of course, Sandy invited me to her church – that church – and I said that I'd think about it. She told me that I was welcome to sit with her family. I went home and I did think about it, but did nothing for months.

Now it was Christmas, and apart from visiting my sisters on Christmas Day, I was alone. I was having some of those black-dog days during Christmas week, feeling abandoned and unconnected. I had nowhere to go, no one to see, no shared history with anyone in Cambridge, so I decided to go to the church on Sunday morning. How bad could it be, anyway? After all, I had nothing to lose, and it would pass a little time on a lonely day. I went and things have never been the same since!

I arrived late, trying to remain unnoticed and sat at the back (easier to hide that way). I was incredibly nervous going into that place. My eyes darted about while I looked for Sandy. I hadn't spoken to her since that course months ago, but now I needed a kind face to turn to. Eventually, I spotted her, sitting closer to the front.

Frankly, I don't remember much about the service. I noticed quickly, though, that it had a different flavour than the Pentecostalism I grew up with. There were screens at the front, coloured lights, and really lively music. It felt loose, fun and alive. When he stood to talk, I recognized David from Glad Tidings in the 80's. I couldn't tell you a thing he said, except he mentioned Sudbury, and somehow that made everything feel alright.

After the service, I found Sandy. She was surprised to see me, and she knew somehow that she should introduce me to David. There was a bunch of people around him, so I waited patiently. But Sandy wasn't so patient. She stepped right into the crowd and said, "David, I've got somebody you should meet."

I stepped forward, shook hands with David, and asked if he remembered me. I could tell he didn't, so I asked if he remembered Tommy Moore. And all of a sudden, he said, "Billy Moore! You're Billy Moore!" It had been years since I had seen him last in Sudbury. I don't know how he could have recognized me. In those days I had long stringy hair and the distinctive look of a head banger. Now here I was in church, sober, straight and in my right mind. He was in shock!

David's Story

I recall the first time I saw Billy. It had been years since I had seen him, and here he was walking up to me in church. It took a moment for my mind to jog, but then I remembered him as if it were yesterday. For years when I was in Sudbury, I prayed for him weekly. I asked God to do a miracle, because I knew how far this puppy had strayed. He was a mess, and I knew how it broke his Dad's heart to see him that way. I'd ask after Billy, and Tommy would choke, hold back the tears, and not say much. All I could tell Tommy was that I was praying for him. And that's what I did. It's funny sometimes how you can pray for someone for a long time – even after you stop believing your prayers are making a difference – years later, you see the miracle you were praying for. That's how it was with Billy!

David asked what I was doing there. I told him my tale of woe (at least the Reader's Digest version) and that I had been clean and sober for almost two years. He was delighted! He took me to meet his wife, Eileen, and she said, "Could you come over for lunch with us?"

I didn't know if I really wanted to go. I had never really known these people and they were treating this like we were long lost friends. And I knew pastors! They probably wanted to get their hooks in me real good. And let's face it, I was shy. I might have been lonely, but I wasn't desperate! I played with the idea in my mind, and took my sweet time getting there. I reluctantly walked up to the door and knocked, and there it was again, that same good-natured friendliness I had hated when I used to drive that guy home from the garage. Only now it felt like warmth, hospitality... genuine friendship.

I made my way into the house, and David introduced me to a friend of his who was visiting from – you guessed it – Sudbury... and would you believe it, he was a guy I partied with in my old life. Mike was the older brother of my buddy Brian's childhood friend, Jimmy. We used to party at Jimmy's house all the time back in the 70's. Jimmy and I grew to be friends on the Crossing Alignment Ball Team, and I had gotten to know Mike partying over there.

I couldn't believe seeing him there at the Pentecostal pastor's house in Cambridge! As we talked, I discovered Mike had become a Christian around the time David had gone to Sudbury, and he struck me as the real deal – a truly devoted follower of Jesus. I was so thrilled to see a familiar face, and it began to play out in my mind what was going on here. Was it just a coincidence that Mike was here on this particular Sunday?

There was one more coincidence to figure out. As we were talking over lunch, David mentioned there was somebody else I should see this weekend. Tim was a guy I had known since childhood. His parents, Tommy and Mike (no, not the first Pentecostal gay couple) – Mike is a nickname for Tim's mother, whose real name was Eileen. They used to spend summer weekends with us on Manitoulin Island. Tim's older brother, Kirk, was my buddy growing up, but he died when he was 29 years old. Tim and I had played hockey on the same team for a while, and of course this included drinking. He had been raised in exactly the same world as I had, and though he was ten years younger, he had taken the same one-way route to oblivion. Last I had seen him, Tim was working in the family business with his dad, and having his own issues with drinking.

But now, lo and behold, here I was at the pastor's house in Cambridge, discovering that Tim, himself, had become a pastor and was running a skid row mission in Ottawa. And he just happened to be staying with David for the weekend, because his son was in a hockey tournament. David hooked me up with Tim, by way of cell phone, and we hung out a bit that afternoon in a Brantford rink. I sat with Tim, his brother-in-law Kent, and his dad, Tommy, as we watched a game and chatted about old times in Sudbury and on Manitoulin Island. Tim shared his story of life transformation and I shared mine, and with tears and hugs, we parted.

Just a couple of coincidences? Or were they God incidents? I was left wondering as I drove home. And I wondered through the week too, until – sure enough – I had wondered my way back to the next Sunday service at Calvary Assembly. I took it as a sign, from God to me, that this is where I should be connected. I had history with these people, and that was something I was looking for. Just the fact that both those guys happened to be there on that Sunday, the day I chose to go to church after procrastinating for so many Sundays, was definitely God saying something loud and clear. There were just too many coincidences in the last little while since I had moved: Ed who gave me my first job and became my first landlord by coincidence, meeting Sandy at the suicide prevention clinic and her connection to Mrs. Nelder and David, and now these amazing meetings with Mike and Tim. God was up to something... I just wasn't sure what.

I began to attend Calvary every Sunday, and that church has become my home. David spent a lot of time with me at first. We got to be friends. We'd hang out, go to a show or just watch some videos at his place or mine. We had a Star Wars extravaganza one time and a Matrix one too. And we had some great talks. David got me up to speed on how the church had changed over the years (it was okay to admit you didn't have it all together) and how it had stayed the same (they still love the Bible and still talk about Jesus a lot!).

When we had become buddies, David felt he could ask for my help. One time he was over at a guy's place when his life was falling apart around him. He called me at work and asked, "Would you be interested in helping someone I know whose wife has just left him with four little kids, and he is struggling with alcohol?" I went over to talk to this guy whose name was Dan, and started by pouring all his beer down the sink. His house was a mess and so was his life. His kids were taken away from him at this point. I started to take him to AA meetings as well as church every Sunday until he was able to get into a Centre. After awhile, with some solid recovery, Dan was able to get his kids back.

During that time, David had encouraged me to join a small group, called Direction for Life. So much of what I had learned as a child came back to me! I knew that the Big Book of AA has twelve promises, but soon realized that the Bible has 7,000! Next, I was in a Bible study group once a week and became very close friends with a few people: Barbara, Sharon, Denise, Prakash, Dan (the guy I was helping), Brian, Heather, Francis, Flo, Gerry, Steve and Irene. Later, most of us did Rick Warren's book The Purpose Driven Life along with a program at church, "40 Days of Purpose", and I began to grow and grow. The book had a chapter for each day of the week, and at the end of the chapter was a practical application to go out and do that day. Each week, the assignments were hard, but I stuck with it. I often talked with my sister Sharon, about the 40 Days of Purpose and how each day mattered so much. She was so enthused that she got a group going at her church.

While studying the Bible, I felt that I should be baptized in water. Every kid in a Pentecostal church knows that other churches baptize babies, but that Pentecostals do it only when you're old enough to make a personal commitment of your life to Christ. And every Pentecostal kid also knows that that's what Mom and Dad want to see more than anything. So, as a dutiful son, I was baptized to make my parents happy, but I didn't have any clue as to the deeper meaning it held. When a believer is baptized, that person is saying, "I identify with Jesus in His death; I, too, want to die to sin and selfishness, and I identify with Jesus in His resurrection! I, too, want to live a new life by the power of the Holy Spirit who is in me!" I went through the motions as a kid, but now, I was a man – a man who was serious about serving the Lord!

And, so, I was baptized on December 1, 2002 with many of my family present. I was told that I had to say a little something about why I wanted to be baptized. It was the first time I ever had to speak in front of so many people. I was so nervous! I told the people that though I was brought up in a Christian home, I had made poor choices and had lost my way. But now I wanted to turn my life over completely to Jesus. Because He died for me, I wanted to live for Him! Just before David immersed me, he told the congregation something I hadn't known before: "While I was living in Sudbury, Billy's Dad had asked me to pray for him. I told him that I would, and I did for many years!" David also said to the congregation, "If anyone out there has a loved one who is not serving the Lord, keep praying for them – miracles do happen and Billy is one of them!" And with tears streaming down his cheeks, he then immersed me and I knew my sins were being washed away.

I wrote in my Journal:

Thank You, God, for bringing me here to Cambridge, to Calvary and to David. You knew it was to be the way that I could make it back to the flock.
I was baptized today. From now on, I'm dedicating my life to You.
Please use me, use my gifts and experiences to help others.
I want to be Your servant and do Your work.
I'm desperate for You.
I'm lost without You.
Please continue to strengthen me in Your ways.

As I got my spiritual and physical life back in order, I realized that I must get my finances straightened out as well. That was a big job – in fact – much bigger than I first expected. But I knew it was something I had to do... kind of like taking responsibility for the life I had lived, and the life I planned to live. The first thing on my radar was back taxes, something

I hadn't really thought about for four years! I phoned my big sister, Sharon, and asked if she would help me to figure out a way to do it.

Sharon said she was heading up to Ottawa to visit friends, so she went right to the taxation office and picked up all the forms I'd need to do my taxes for the last four years. The most recent form was easy... I had all the information for 2001, and, frankly, it wasn't much. But each year before that became a little harder to work on. The worst year, though, was 1998 (the last year I owned Crossing Alignment). Not only had I lost all the documentation – let's face it – my memory wasn't particularly reliable either.

Truth is, I had left the shop in Sudbury and walked away with nothing. It was a bad time. My addictions had taken over. Things with Ellen were in shambles. I hardly showed up for work, and when I did, there was a mounting pile of bills to meet me. I had long since stopped paying Sharon the money I owed her. I was full of excuses and it just seemed easier to hit the bar and drink beer with the hollow-eyed rubbies. After all, I was becoming one myself.

The new owner, my old manager and friend, Paul, had thrown all my stuff out. I had nothing to work with for my tax return, so I just told the truth. I wrote that I had no record of how much I had made that year. I knew that I took gas, food and apartment money from the business. I guessed $250 cash a week. I told them that I had gone to rehab and couldn't remember anything else. Then I signed the forms and sent them off to the taxation office.

I anxiously awaited to hear back from them. None of my dealings with the government (while I was in business) had been good, so I didn't look forward to the reply. One day, I came home from work and found a letter from Revenue Canada in the mail. Big gulp. My heart sank and jumped all at the same time. Why? Because on the one hand, I wasn't sure just how bad the news could be. On the other, I was so proud of myself for facing the music. My tendency would have been to put the letter down, then walk around it a few times and wonder, and then finally open it – or maybe not open it at all for a long time. But I was in recovery! I had learned the importance of dealing with reality for what it is, knowing there's nothing that my higher power and I can't face together! Since I had surrendered my life to Christ, that conviction was even stronger, so I tore open that letter and read it.

My response to reading the letter was complete shock! The reply was a surprise! Far from levying heavy fines or exacting a huge toll, they accepted all I had said at face value, and I even received a few dollars back! That was a HUGE load off my shoulders! I immediately got on the blower and phoned Sharon. All she could say was, "Thank God!" I guess it was as big a deal to her as it was to me. Ever since then, I continue to file – on time – every year.

Money was something that I never could handle. So I started with baby steps. I made envelopes with labels on them, like rent, phone, cable, heat, insurance, etc. It was primitive alright, but it was the only way I could do it. I didn't even write cheques or use my bank card! I was simply petrified of losing track of it all over again. If I saw the money going into a certain envelope, I could understand that that's where it stayed until I paid that bill, and I would see it coming out of my hand. It was simple, but it worked at the time. I don't do that anymore, since I've graduated to a more sophisticated accounting system: the shoebox. Not really, but I keep everything on a calendar and do it all online, now. So far, so good! I can even trust myself with a credit card now! Those cards got me in a lot of trouble in the past, but I only buy things I have the money for, and pay the bill monthly.

Calling Sharon into the tax matter though, set a whole other issue into motion that I hadn't considered at all. Neither Sharon nor Ken had ever spoken a word about it to me personally, but I became aware that I had cost them a large sum of money – large enough that it was painful to hear, and almost impossible to correct. After all the tax stuff was dealt with, I stirred up enough courage to broach the subject with my sister. It wasn't easy for either of us, but we settled on a payment scheme that would honour the debt, and was manageable for me. The sum I paid them back monthly was a pittance, but meant real sacrifice for me, especially in those early days. I think Sharon and Ken were proud of me for addressing the issue, but after seven years of paying them back, they wrote me a letter explaining the principal of the Sabbath. The Old Testament (Deuteronomy 15:1-2) had a principal of releasing debtors from their debts every seventh year, so Sharon and Ken chose to release me of mine. I had always been grateful for Sharon and Ken's love and help, especially after I began to understand how far they went to show it. But ever since the day I received that letter, I have been grateful and free! Grateful feels good, but grateful and free is out of this world!

Soon, I began to work with the youth at my church. This was quite a change for me, as I am naturally quiet and an introvert. That's one of the reasons for the drugs and alcohol: to be more outgoing! I was now a helper with young teens.

Chapter 14:
Redemption

redeem:
1. buy back; recover by expenditure of effort or by a stipulated payment.
2. make a single payment to discharge (a regular charge or obligation).
3. convert (tickets, bonds etc.) into goods or cash.
4. *Theol.* deliver from sin and damnation.
5. make up for; be a compensating factor in.
6. (*foll.* by from) save from (a defect).
7. *refl.* compensate for past failings, esp. so as to regain favour.
8. save (a person's life) by ransom.
9. save or rescue or reclaim.
10. fulfill (a promise).

Source: Oxford Canadian Dictionary, Second Edition

A question you wonder about when you've been an abuser of various substances for twenty-seven years, is whether there's any way to redeem the years you've lost. Is there any good that can come from that cesspool, or is it completely a lost cause, an abyss of darkness, a complete dead end? I wasn't sure, even after I had given control of my life over to Jesus. It took awhile to discover that one of the things He delights in is the business of turning garbage into gold! I guess that's what God calls 'redemption'.

The Bible says that our tears are precious to God (Psalm 56:8). God loves to take our brokenness and turn it into healing for others. I am convinced that nothing is ever wasted in God's kingdom, not even the wasted years of my life... and wasted in more ways than one! He always finds ways to restore what we've lost (Joel 2:25). All things, even our profoundest stupidities, work together for good when we love the Lord (Romans 8:28).

So in a strange twist, that race truck of mine became a pivotal part of the story. It started with one of my long chats with David... it could have been over dinner at his place or after a movie, but one day David casually mentioned I should get involved at the church somehow. It was nice to come on Sundays, but sitting like a couch potato in front of a talking head wasn't God's idea of radical Christian living! We kicked the idea around for a bit and then he suggested I should work with Junior Highs. Of course, I didn't realize at the time that this was a suicide assignment. Grades 6 to 8 were a disaster for me personally; I was about to discover they're not easy for anybody! On the other hand, I knew how formative this period was, how sensitive kids' hearts are at that age, beneath the rough-and-tumble exterior.

I decided to try it out, as long as I could hang in the background... way in the background, where I could remain uninvolved in any serious way. I didn't want to be centred out – just wanted to blend in with the other leaders and be a glorified baby-sitter. So I showed up on a Wednesday evening and was fairly mobbed by about seventy 'tweens', some from the church, but most community kids.

They all had energy, and none of them seemed to notice or mind that someone new had showed up; they were wired for sound. A few of them pushed the envelope with me to see if I would crack, but I held my ground pretty good. What happened to hanging way back? I was soon in there, like a dirty shirt, building relationships – especially with the church kids I saw on Sundays. It touched my heart to know I was there working with kids who were just about the age I was when I was deciding to leave God and the church behind.

I wondered about what you could do to keep kids that age interested in church. When I was one of them, our church seemed to have nothing fun for us to do. Part of my young rebellion was to hate the "official" church activities, like skating or bowling and young people's meetings that were just like church. So I kept thinking about how to catch their interest to keep them coming.

I worked hard at getting to know these kids, but there just seemed to be an insurmountable wall between us. One day, I was over at David's house with my race truck (on a tow bar) behind my old Suburban that I had recently purchased. David's son Jonny, and a buddy of his from the group named Cam were there. They took one look at the old S10 and they freaked out!

"Wow, do you race that thing?"

"Yeah."

"Can we watch?"

"Well, it's been awhile… Anyway, first I'm going to have to work on it to finish getting it ready…" I saw their interest, so I hopped into the driver's seat and fired it up. The 600 horsepower 454 came alive with a loud roar from the open headers. It was deafening to hear, and the boys loved it.

"Can we come when you race it?" they chimed.

I knew I had them. Of course that kind of enthusiasm is what
cranks kids, especially at that age. Anyone who's ever tried
to pull a group of 11 to 14 year olds into an effective pit crew
knows it can be pandemonium! At first, it was just Jonny
and Cam who came to help me out, but after the Junior High
Pastor had me tell my life story to the whole group, I managed to pick up a lot of interest. Soon I had a willing crew of
teens, and they wanted to help me get back into racing! They
would come with me to competitions, help change tires and
unload stuff, and basically have a great time. We raced as
much as I could afford to. We even won a few races, and that
paid for more entry fees. A few years earlier, when I had lost
everything, I couldn't get rid of that truck, not even for a few
badly needed dollars. Now it was turning out to be the best
tool I could find to work with kids!

The Waterloo Regional Police, along with the RCMP, put
on a special motor sport event every year. It's called Racing
Against Drugs. They invite race cars from all over for show.
People gather to see them, touch them and get their picture
taken with them. Along with the cars, they have all these
awareness booths set up. Some are about drugs, others about
smoking and others deal with alcohol; even MADD (Mothers
Against Drunk Driving) attend. The police bring their roll-
over simulator, showing you what happens to your body in
a car crash. They even have a drunk-driving simulator. The
whole thing is aimed at preteens. Every day, they bring Grade
6 classes through, and the kids learn so much, spending a few
minutes at each interactive booth. One night of the week, it's
open to the public and has lots of activities going on.

In 2003, I was able to get my truck in the car show. The day before the show, my truck was in mud races up in Sudbury. I had been back a few times before this… and it wasn't easy. In fact, to this day, Sudbury is a hard place for me to go back to. There are a lot of painful memories there, on every corner, it seems. I did have a lot of good years there, but I seem to only remember the bad ones. Each time I return is a little better than the last.

I thought I should tell the announcer at the Sudbury Mud Races that I was "Racing Against Drugs," and that the next day I was headed to Cambridge for the Racing Against Drugs Car Show for the week. It turned out the announcer was a recovering alcoholic. "I've been in AA twenty years," he said. "I'm right behind you!" Then for the rest of the day, every time my truck was on deck, he'd announce, "Billy Moore… Racing Against Drugs… and can you believe this truck is going to be in a Car Show in Cambridge at 7:00 a.m. tomorrow morning?!"

A lot of my old drinking and drug buddies were there, and they had a hard time believing it was me. I did take some time to chat with them, and we had some good laughs. It's hard to say what they made of it all. The parents of a long-time rival racer came and talked to me. They had seen me at my worst – wired and bent out of shape. The mother started crying as she told me how happy she was for me.

I left Sudbury at eleven that night, after a gruelling day of racing, where I managed to take home some hardware and win a bit of cash – just enough to cover my expenses for the weekend! By the end of the day, the truck literally had two inches of mud, top to bottom, caked on inside and out. I washed that truck down four times before I left, and when I got home at five in the morning, I waxed and polished it until I took it to the show at seven in the morning.

Only a few vehicles were selected for the Racing Against Drugs Car Show, held at the indoor rink in the Cambridge Mall, and mine was one. It stayed there for the entire week, and many kids got to see it, and other race cars up close. I've been in that show four times. From then on, at all the races, we were branded. "Racing Against Drugs" was our motto, and all the track announcers picked up on it and made a big deal out of it. I think we got known!

After that, a buddy of mine named Tony and I built another truck for Tough Truck races, painted exactly the same. For you novices, Tough Trucks are regular pick-up trucks with tricked out suspensions, made for jumping and cornering at high speeds. Mine is an '87 Ford Ranger with a 2.3-4 cylinder engine. With it, I've been able to attend events at the Roger's Centre in Toronto and Copps Coliseum in Hamilton, as well as a whole bunch of smaller fairs and races. We made it to about ten different races a year, all over Ontario. My Junior High "pit crew" looked great in their "Racing Against Drugs" t-shirts, and along the way, we got a few chances to tell people who we were and why we did it.

During that time, we'd have a special night at the church with all the youth, called "Racing Against Drugs" night. We'd bring both my trucks to the church, and park them right at the front doors where the youth enter. I'd do a talk on drugs, a different one every year, and then we'd all go outside and make some noise! I'd do some burnouts and donuts and stuff with one truck, and we even built a jump for the other truck to jump. I loved the chance to give kids, who I'd built a bit of a relationship with, the straight scoop on drugs. You can read what I told them in the next chapter.

Now it was time to get something cool to drive on the street, but I needed to do it properly and not let it become an obsession again. I would give myself permission to do it if I could afford to (and still pay all my bills on time!). I told you, I'm a car nut. My old friend, Ernie and I decided to customize my Suburban (okay, I actually had to talk him into it – and I couldn't use dope to persuade him. For the first time in recorded history, it actually cost me money to get him to work on my truck!).

So I took the Suburban up to Sudbury for the winter, and Ernie went at it. Next time I saw it, the roof was chopped, or lowered six inches. Later, the suspension was lowered about six inches, too. It took a couple of years, on and off, and still isn't completely finished (they never are!), but I love it just the same. It attracts a lot of attention (uh oh? Here we go again!). Wherever I go (especially at the races) when I am pulling one of my off-road trucks to an event, I'm not sure what it is about me that likes that kind of attention – but I do – and I'm really not sure it's altogether healthy. I'm trying to find the balance on that issue, but I will say this much… It feels good to be able to know that I was able to get this done without getting high or drunk even once! Not so sure I could say that about old buddy, Ernie!

At one of the racing events I went to at Copps Coliseum in Hamilton, Pastor David and Eileen came out to watch and cheer me on. After my race, they had a demolition derby. David seemed to enjoy it so much. As he was laughing and shouting, I got a brainwave… wouldn't it be great to turn this into a church project? So I asked him if he had ever wanted to drive one of those cars. (It crossed my mind, because – as holy and reverent as the sainted man is – he does have a reputation for being rough on his vehicles). "Sure," he said. "I've always wished I could bust a few cars at no cost and without the insurance issues!" So I tucked the idea in the back of my head, knowing it would come back in its own time.

So the next spring, I pulled together a bunch of the kids that had been helping me at the races, both girls and guys. I donated my $500 beater that I first bought when I moved to Cambridge. Doug, a contractor in our church, had lots of garage space – so he donated a place to work on it and the equipment we would need. Those kids began ripping that car apart with incredible fervour. For a few hours, every Friday night that summer, we'd get together and work on it. A lot has to be done to make a car into a demolition derby car, and there are a ton of rules to follow. Those kids learned how to use all kinds of tools. They discovered what holds a car together, and how to take one apart. By summer's end, we painted it up and it was ready to go!

We got it done in time for the Cambridge Fall Fair, and entered it in the derby. Of course, David was the driver – and given his reputation – we came up with the ominous moniker: THE PASTOR OF DISASTOR! which we painted on the roof. Half the church showed up to cheer him on. And when the cars paraded in for the "Best Looking Car of the Night" contest (decided by audience applause), our car won the trophy hands down! Although it didn't last too long in the demolition derby, we all had a great time.

The next two years, the kids designed and painted a couple of other cars. One was based on the movie Finding Nemo – the other on The Incredibles – and we won the best looking car every time. David got better each year – and so did the cars – but we still haven't made it to the end. The car always seems to die before it should.

I also was able to get the same kids to build four soap box derby cars. We got the kits, and they put them all together and painted them. They are really cool. We invite all the smaller kids, ages 5 to 11 from the church and the community, to participate. All they need is a helmet; everything else is supplied. There is a nice-sized hill entering the parking lot of the church, and that becomes the race track every year on a Saturday in August. The church supplies trophies, and gifts are donated from local businesses. We even have a free barbeque. There's a host of volunteers who help every year, and at each running the race gets bigger. Last time we had ninety-six competitors!

In the first three years, the girls won them all. Some kids get a little disappointed when they don't win, but I think that is a good life lesson. Just because you don't always win at everything you do, doesn't mean you can't have a little fun along the way! It has become an annual event at the church, and we're all pretty proud of it.

As Calvary became more and more my church home, I noticed something was missing. I had benefited so much from the help of Bill W. and Dr. Bob, the originators of AA. I wondered if there was a more Christ-centered approach that the church could use to create a place for broken people to put their lives together. All the Sunday stuff and the extracurricular stuff at Calvary is great. But when you're wounded – deeply broken – you need something more.

I began to search for a program like that, and discovered Celebrate Recovery. It is a twelve-step, Christian-based recovery program that was started by John Baker of Saddleback church in California (Rick Warren's church). It is for all hurts, habits and hang-ups. We wrote away and received the start-up package. I was very excited to begin this new venture. It was to expand from there to include a worship band and speakers every week before we broke off into groups. We began with a men's group of ten and met one night a week at the church. This program involves prayer, the Twelve Steps along with a corresponding Bible verse for each step, a reading, plus a workbook which lasts for one year. This program has no anonymity, after all, it is called "Celebrate Recovery" and many people did not want to announce that they had problems by showing up every Monday night. It only lasted for a year and slowly dissolved (to my disappointment), but it's just like Jesus to raise things from the dead. Over the last year at Calvary, Celebrate Recovery has become a reality, and broken people of all sorts are finding love, acceptance and forgiveness in Christ and the kind of freedom I've been enjoying for ten years now!

redeem

I love that word: redemption. I've been absolutely awed by the fact that the Lord has taken some of the things that had almost destroyed me, and has turned them into channels of healing and wholeness. I'm thrilled that God changed my life into something so much better than it used to be; that He 'offset the bad effects' of my former life and found a way to make them worthwhile in my new life!

Chapter 15:
The 411 – Talking to Kids About Reality

So, given the chance… This is what I actually say to teens and tweens: Chances are that many of them will try drugs and alcohol. I try to make them aware of what can happen (if that is their choice). I am not too concerned with what they become… a doctor, a lawyer, an engineer, a janitor, a waitress, a taxi driver... what I am concerned about is what they don't become... an alcoholic or a drug addict! It's not a good career – and the fringe benefits last a lifetime!

FIRST, alcohol is a drug. Alcohol and drug addiction is hereditary – it is in your genes. This means that if someone in your family – even a distant relative such as an aunt, uncle, grandparent or great-grandparent – had or has a problem with drugs and/or alcohol, you probably will, too. I had two uncles and two first cousins who were much older than me, who were all alcoholics. One of them had a son who died from an accidental drug overdose at the age of 28. It might not happen right away – it might take years – but it could very well happen to you. Addictions are slow and progressive. Even if it's not in your family, if you start to use drugs and alcohol regularly, you will get hooked! They are very addictive substances. The saying goes, "If you play with fire, you will get burned." It's the same with drugs and alcohol. The longer you play with them, the more damage you will do – not only to yourself, but to others around you… the people who care for you, and love you!

You can get hooked and you don't even see it coming until it is too late! That's what happened to me. You will definitely pay the price, one way or another, when you play with drugs and alcohol. And the more you play with them, the higher the price gets!

TV, the movies and the music you listen to all glorify drugs and alcohol. It's cool; it's so much fun. But they never, ever show or tell you what it's like after the fun is over... the sickness, the pain and suffering that you put yourself and others through! They never talk about the money you waste – all on a temporary feeling and some artificial joy – none of it is real.

I know that I can't stop anyone from doing drugs or drinking alcohol; no one can stop you if you make the choice to try it. And I know that if and when you become addicted, you can't even stop yourself! But, here's the kicker... you can choose not to start!

The opposite of "high" is "low". Let me tell you that the higher you get the night before, the lower you'll feel the morning after! Guilt, shame and remorse eventually set in – not when you first begin – no, you feel great when you think you're just playing around; it's after you can't get out of the cycle that negative feelings come over you. It all comes from that sense of powerlessness to help yourself and that dim awareness that you may have said or done something that you can't recall or take back.

I'm not trying to tell you that everyone that has a drink or smokes a joint becomes addicted, but millions of people do! As far as pot (marijuana) is concerned, it will almost always lead you to harder drugs, which become more addictive more quickly. That's what happened to me. It is said that marijuana is a "soft" drug, but marijuana contains 460 chemicals. When it is smoked, these increase to 2,000 chemicals! A study of fifty teenagers who got stoned at least twice a week for four months, found that their brain movements were immature for their age and showed signs of impairment. When challenged, all of the students had trouble doing simple academic tasks. Their brains just didn't act normally. The reason for this is that THC, the active ingredient in marijuana, actually binds to the fatty tissues of your brain and blocks the receptors. Little wonder that after using for a few years, people notice your brain doesn't work as well as it used to! The THC level today is over 25% greater than it used to be. If marijuana was proven to be harmful a long time ago, what is it now when it's even more potent?

Cocaine became a part of my life, too. Not only is it very expensive, but it seems like you can never get enough. It tightens the body's blood vessels and raises the blood pressure as much as 20% above normal. This increases the danger of a brain hemorrhage. It increases the heart rate and in some cases, sudden death occurs – even on the first usage. It also tends to release inhibitions so that the user acts in ways he or she wouldn't normally act. When the high wears off, the user feels restless, quarrelsome, depressed, fatigued, lazy and unable to concentrate. Once you start, it's easy to spend $200 in a few hours. In just a couple of years, I blew multiplied tens of thousands of dollars with nothing to show for it – except the things it took away from me!

These are all facts based on things I had researched and heard at the time (when I first starting working with teenagers years ago), below are some of my personal interpretations of how many teens can get hooked on alcohol and drugs:

Since 9 out of 10 teens will experiment with drugs and alcohol:

- 3 of those 9 teens will become addicted
- 1 of those 3 teens will die from a drug or alcohol related death, overdose or accident

Which one of those kids would you prefer to be if you could choose? It is your choice! Which path will you take? One will definitely lead you to self-destruction. This is the one path the devil wants you to take. He wants to see you fail! The other path (with God's help) might not be easy, might not always be fun, might seem like you are missing out on other things and will not be perfect – BUT – it will be worth it, because God has promised it will be!

So you have got to ask yourself, do I take the chance of wrecking all of my dreams and goals, and possibly end in an early death due to an overdose or an accident, or just being in the wrong place at the wrong time with the wrong people? Let me tell you about my friend, Rockie. I used to hang around a bar where a biker gang went. One day, three of the biggest, baddest, bikers you ever did see, came into the bar. They decided that they didn't like the look of Rockie, so they proceeded to drag him out of the bar and beat him within an inch of his life. They broke his leg, broke his ribs, and left him with massive head injuries. The good news is that he lived. The bad news is... he has never fully recovered. It could have been me just as easily. Why wasn't it? I don't know. Maybe God was watching over me...

What's scary is that you don't get here overnight. I didn't just wake up one morning and say, "I think I'm going to become an alcoholic and a drug addict today." But it happened in time, after I had made the choice to try it.

I didn't want to make enemies out of friends.
I didn't want to lose my wife and son.
I didn't want to fail at my business and go bankrupt.
I didn't want to have my sisters give up on me.
I didn't want to lose all my material possessions.
And I sure didn't want to lose my dog, Winston…

But… it all happened! It all happened after I made the choice to do drugs and alcohol, and then they took over my life! First, I took a drink and a toke, and then, they took me! They took me places I didn't want to go. It's only by the grace of God, that I was able to kick those habits! I have no desire to take a drink or do drugs today. With a lot of hard work and God's help, I've been relieved of those obsessions.

Here are a few things I've learned: I can tell you that everyone has a gift. Some are good at school; some are good at sports; some are good at music; some are good at building things; some may not know what they are good at yet, but keep trying and you will find it eventually! Everyone is important! There is no one else exactly like you in the entire world. You are exactly the way God wanted you to be. Everything about you is unique. Everything about you makes you who you are – and you are okay! So…

Believe in yourself.

Say "NO" to drugs.

Make the right choices so you'll have good consequences.

Don't give up on what you want the most… for what you want at the moment.

Being a 'church kid' doesn't guarantee that you will make it through the teen years easily, but having a personal relationship with Jesus will help! So will reading your Bible! You know what Bible stands for, don't you?

B – basic
I – instruction
B – before
L – leaving
E – earth

You see, I've discovered that you don't have to get high to be high! I never understood that for so long! The simplest "highs" in life are free. It is so simple! I'm high on life – with God's help. Also, with God's help, I've been able to rebuild my life. I've been given a second chance! So many of my friends are still stuck where I was.

After seeing the movie The Matrix, I saw all kinds of parallels to the "drug life". In the movie, the main character, Neo, thinks he is in the real world, until he gets unplugged: disconnected from the artificial computer-generated matrix that gave him the illusion of life. Everything looked better, tasted better, felt better in the matrix, but it wasn't real. Life outside the matrix was hard, rough, challenging – but at least it was real life. While I was living the high life, I was sure that was the real life. That's how everyone feels. But when I got out and took a step back, I could see that the matrix of drugs and alcohol had deceived me; I thought it was all good, but it had left devastation in its wake... how come I couldn't see that before? How come I couldn't see my wife's tears or hear my son crying out for Dad? How come I couldn't recognize the pain in my mom's eyes, and the betrayal in my Dad's heart? Why was I so oblivious to what was happening to my business? All of it was caught up in the deception of my personal matrix of beer and dope! But to extend the movie metaphor: I chose the red pill, I chose the truth… and the truth really did set me free! I can now see that none of that matrix life was really life at all!

To this day, when I catch up with old buddies and they happen to be having a few beers or sharing a joint, I see them plugging into the matrix as clear as day, even if they don't notice it themselves. They seem to leave you behind; you're no longer part of their world. A few minutes ago, you were all having a great time together, but now something's changed. Now, what's funny to them isn't as humorous to you. What matters to them, isn't so significant for you, and what you think is of earth-shattering importance, they think is inconsequential. They've disappeared into the matrix. Some come and go. Others just seem to live there – like I did for so many years. And a few – very few – make it back. I thank God I did. All I can do is pray for my friends and show them my changed life.

Several years ago, God reached out and rescued me. Ten years ago, I gave my heart to Him! He slowly began to work in my life. He has opened my eyes to see that being a Christian can be a lot of fun! Good things have happened since I made that choice! God has helped me achieve things that I never thought I could. I'm working with teens and racing both mud trucks and tough trucks all over Ontario; speaking at different groups of all ages, telling them my story. Like it says in the Bible (Ps. 37:4), it turns out God really does give you the desires of your heart.

Back when Ken and Sharon pulled the plug on me, I was absolutely devastated. As I watched them sell my Dad's business to my buddy, Paul, for a song, I recall Ken saying,

"You'll thank us someday for this." I didn't think so. I could never imagine thanking Ken and Sharon for snatching my livelihood from under me. I was mad, humiliated and at the end of my rope.

But in the end, Sharon and Ken did the best thing for me. It was painful and it wasn't easy to say the least, but it set everything in motion that made me what I am today. But now, I do thank them for what they did. I never would have gotten out of that mess on my own; I would never have discovered sanity; I would never have recovered my soul, and I would never get to see my parents in heaven. But because they were willing to embrace 'tough love', I am becoming the person I was meant to be.

My solution to the crisis of my life would have been finding a loonie while walking down the street, buying a lottery ticket with it and discovering that I had won ten million dollars. That's how I would have preferred it, but God had a different plan for me, and it wasn't the way I would have chosen. As usual, I took the long way around… the scenic tour… but it's turned out to be the best way for me.

Chapter 16:
The Award

One day in the winter of 2004, my phone rang. At the other end was a friend from church, Sheryll. She's the lady I had gone out with a few times, but it was settled pretty quickly that we'd be better friends than anything else.

"Hey, Billy. Have you ever heard of the 'The Courage to Come Back' award?"

"Is that some kind of racing trophy?" I asked, not really listening.

"No, stupid, it's an award that is given by the Centre for Addiction and Mental Health in Toronto (CAMH). They find seven Canadians every year who have the "courage to come back" from mental illness or depression or addiction. They're looking for people who've turned their lives around and are making a difference in their community, and I thought of you!"

"Huh? Are you talking to me? What kind of a difference do you suppose I make? I'm not the mayor or the police chief. I haven't seen my name in the papers. I'm just a regular guy struggling to get through every day."

"Well, maybe that's how you see it, but it's not how the rest of us see it. You're a miracle, Billy! Look where you've come from, and look at what you're doing. I think you're kind of a hometown hero."

She proceeded to inform me that she had decided to enter my name to CAMH for one of the awards. I tried to argue with her, but you know Sheryll. Well, you don't, but you probably know somebody like her. I was a bit apprehensive, but I figured why not let her do it? I didn't think I was anyone special (and still don't), but she'll feel like she did something nice for me, and that'll be the end of it.

The next day, with my Pastor David's help, she wrote a letter nominating me and sent it off. There were over eighty other candidates from all over Ontario. A few months later, I got another phone call. This time it wasn't Sheryll, but a woman I didn't know.

"Hello. Is this Billy Moore?"

"Uh... yeah?" There was a little uncertainty in my voice.

Then she introduced herself as Bonnie, the Senior Development Officer for CAMH. I'd kind of forgotten about the whole award thing, so it didn't immediately click what this was about... but half a second later, I remembered and thought: so here's the Dear John call. Thanks for coming out buddy, but we have bigger fish to fry. And that was just fine with me. After all, I'm just small fry anyway. But before I could say, "Oh yeah..." She went on.

"I just wanted to congratulate you on being one of the seven recipients of this year's Courage to Come Back Award!"

My first reaction was "Huh?" My next response was "Well, that's nice." I'll get a letter and a little scroll to hang with my racing trophies, and we'll all live happily ever after. Again, before I could say thank you, Bonnie began to unfold what this award involved.

"You'll be getting a call in the next few days from your local media, and in the next week or so, the Toronto Sun will be running a spread on the recipients. Our film crew will be in to put together a video for the award night, and oh, by the way, you'll have to give an acceptance speech before a thousand people at a thousand-dollar-a-plate gala event."

Now my head was swimming. "Huh? What? Did you say speech? Video? What? News... paper...?" Now I'm wondering what did I get myself into. Wait until I get my hands on Sheryll! What the...?

"Don't worry, Billy," came the reassuring voice on the other end. "We'll walk you through it, and help with each detail. I just wanted to be the first to let you know." With a bit of calm persuasion, she managed to talk me off the ledge. By the end of the call, I was even starting to like the idea. I didn't know how I was going to do it, but I knew I was going to do it!

A whirlwind of events began to unfold! First, CAMH came to Cambridge with a camera crew, and did an interview with me for the banquet. I was asked to share a little of my story. This was fairly easy, because we did the interview at the church and I felt comfortable there. It was also being taped, Bonnie said, so don't worry if you mess up... they'll fix it." The team also wanted some tapes of my racing, as well as a tape of all the kids working on the demolition derby car to edit into the story.

Then, there was a little lull in the action. The CAMH team touched base with me from time to time about all the details of the big night. I could invite five (count 'em, five only!) people. I asked if I could buy another plate, but Bonnie told me our table was sponsored by Merrill Lynch, at a cost of $10,000! And we were talking about a major social event. We'd be hobnobbing with the rich and famous! Real live celebrities, corporate CEOs, political bigwigs. In fact, one of the recipients was the honourable James Bartleman, Lieutenant Governor of Ontario! About a week away, it all started to sink in big time!

Then the local Cambridge paper came to my place and did an interview with me. A couple of days later, there it was... a huge colour picture of me, standing beside my race truck on the front page of the paper with the interview.

Next, the Kitchener paper came to my work and did the same thing. The Toronto Sun even did an article on me, along with all the other recipients of the award. David made a big thing of it at church on Sunday. I was even stopped in the streets by those who recognized me! But that was only the appetizer...

The big day was rapidly approaching. I had to go buy a new suit and all the accessories to go along with it. I was getting nervous. I was working on my speech, wondering how I would ever do it. Talking to fifty junior highs was hard enough... but a thousand or more people in tuxes and evening gowns? The Weston Harbour Castle, in Toronto? And it was going to be televised by Rogers Television? Am I really going to be able to pull this off?

The day had arrived, and I was a bundle of nerves. I had invited Sheryll to accompany me. After all, it was her vision and imagination that got us here, though I still wasn't sure at this point whether to thank her or cuss her. We are good friends, but we argue a lot, something like brother and sister.

We were told to be there early in the afternoon to rehearse our speeches and meet all the other recipients. That part was okay, since not too many people were there yet. But as the time approached, the media began to flock the award winners. First, a picture here with this dignitary and then another with some other VIP. I met so many high ranking society people, I can't remember any of them. At one point, it felt like the Academy Awards with so many flashes going off, one after another! All that attention was overwhelming!

It was lining up to be one of the scariest nights of my life. Sheryll, Pastor David Courey, my sisters Ardith and Sharon and my son, Tyler were all there to support me for my big moment. It was so meaningful for me that Tyler had come. Truth be told, though, I couldn't tell you a thing about the meal. They might as well have given me a cheese sandwich.

On either side of the stage there were huge screens. When we were introduced one at a time, parts of the interview and pictures from our lives, were shown on the big screens. There were Tommy and Elaine Moore; Little Billy and his sisters; a picture of me and my bud, Coop, with long hair, posing and looking up at the sky outside Jean's and my first apartment; Tyler as a baby; hockey pictures and a racing video; kids working on the crash-up cars, and the soap box derby. It was a kaleidoscope of my life, and each image evoked so much emotion. Each presentation showed what we were and what we had now become. The interesting thing was that five of the seven said that the change had only happened because God intervened in their lives and turned them around! That was certainly my story!

I was fifth to go up on stage. It was torture to wait and watch all the others tell their stories. I'd try to listen to them, and as I did, I'd wonder, "What am I doing here? Their story is so much better than mine." But, to be honest, it was hard to concentrate, and I don't remember much of what they said; I just kept rehearsing my speech in my head. David leaned over and asked, "You nervous?" (as if it didn't show!)

"Yeah," I said, breathless.

"Don't worry, I still get nervous every Sunday. You'll do great!"

Rob, the guy from Merrill Lynch said, "Come on Billy, this is easy. You've already done the hardest thing in your life! You beat your addiction and went through the harrowing experience of getting free. This is a piece of cake!"

My name was finally called. The video began with me racing my truck, flying down the track, then working with the kids on the demolition derby car. My legs felt like rubber as I made my way to the stage. I've said that I'm quiet and introverted; now I was in front of 1,500 well-dressed, well-educated businessmen, the other award winners and their families, giving my acceptance speech. I took a deep breath and started. Here's what I actually said:

"I want to thank CAMH and my sponsor, Merrill Lynch. I'm more used to speaking to a bunch of kids than a crowd like this, but here it goes anyway!

"I know that there are many more people out there that deserve this award more than I do. My recovery has been based on giving back to God and society for all the wrongs that I have done. So to receive an award for it, just seems weird to me.

"There are a lot of people I need to thank. To my friend, Sheryll, thanks for nominating me, to my sisters, Sharon and Ardith, thank you for your love and prayers, even in the worst of times. To my son, Tyler, thank you for letting me back into your life. To Pastor David and his wife Eileen, for giving me the odd push to get out of my comfort zone. To Hailey and Beth from the addiction counselling facility in Kitchener, for giving me a lot more tools to survive in my world without drugs and alcohol, but mostly to God for giving me a second chance.

"I know I'm not where I should be yet...... But thank God, I'm not where I once was! So, I'll close with what I like to tell all the kids: you don't have to get high to be high, and believe in yourself and say no to drugs... Thank you very much."

Done! It wasn't so bad, actually. In fact, I felt like I'd done pretty well! It helped that, with all the bright lights, I couldn't see a soul out there! But when I finished, the applause was deafening.

I was then escorted to the side of the stage where my sponsor was. He presented me with this large, glass book. It was standing with the pages open and there was engraving on every page about courage. On the last page it said, "The award formed of glass symbolizes how vulnerable and fragile the human spirit can be. Yet when framed with courage and dignity, it is inspiring in its strength and beauty."

More pictures were taken on stage. I was blinded, and found it difficult to navigate my way back to my seat. At least, now,

I was able to enjoy the rest of the evening, surrounded by my loved ones. It was a high that I had never experienced before, not even from any drug! It was real, and by now, I loved the moment – my fifteen minutes of fame!

Although my time in the spotlight was over, I did receive invitations to appear at different places. Like the Discovery Health Channel, who invited me to participate in a show called Health on the Line with Avery Hines. My story was shown on tape and then I was brought out. The show was what they call "live to air" – recorded live and unedited for broadcast. I was on a discussion panel with three doctors, and another guy who had received the same award I did, but he was a radio personality. It was very nerve-wracking and I couldn't get a word in edgewise, even if I wanted to. I was also asked to do a little promotion for an addiction counsel-ling facility in Kitchener on the local television network. I gladly agreed, because of all they had done for me. This was no problem; it was taped and was one on one, where I find I do a lot better. I never did see it, but I was told it was good.

A Christian singles group also asked me to come and share my story. Now these are adults, and I have a bit of a problem standing up in front of them! So I just brought some video footage. It was professionally done, and told my story better than I could have by myself. Then I took questions for awhile and got into more detail about a lot of things, as I tried to explain how someone addicted to drugs and alcohol thinks, and justifies their actions.

Something good came out of that, too. A woman was there named Donna. I told my friend, Sheryll, that I wanted to meet her. So good ole Sheryll set us up. Donna was hesitant about getting to know me, because she had been burned by someone with addictions before – someone she trusted and thought that I just might do that, too. Although we spent a lot of time together over the next five years, it was not to be and I began to see myself alone forever. Maybe that was what God wanted.

At that time I was living in a pretty nice apartment, but I was paying huge rent. I decided that I should check into what it would take to buy a little house and not keep paying some-one else's mortgage. So I began making some calls and found out that I now had the best credit rating a person could have. This blew my mind! I had never ever had good credit in the past and had totally given up on ever having any. However, being responsible and paying all my bills on time for over ten years really paid off. Now I had possibilities.

Next came jumping through all the hoops, with all the red tape and paperwork involved in the process of buying a house. I was finally approved, and because I had been putting money into RRSPs for a few years, I even had enough for a down payment.

I found a nice little house in the area close to my work and bought it without any help from anyone. This was a great accomplishment for me. Not only to buy the house, but to muddle through all that paper work and get it done right.

Now I had a nice little house to tinker around and fix up, but I realized that there was really something missing… someone to share it with and make it a home.

THEN IT HAPPENED

I can remember telling someone at church over nine years ago, as I pointed to the front doors of the church and said, "The woman of my dreams will walk through those doors any day now." I think it was more of a joke than a prophecy – and I wanted to believe it – but as the years went on, it was like another unanswered prayer that fades away. Then when you are just becoming to realize your fate of being alone for the rest of your life, God shines his light on you, and there she is!

I first saw Monique in the fall of 2010. I noticed her while I was having my Sunday coffee at the church coffee shop after the first service. She came to the late service and quickly made her way through the foyer to the sanctuary. I found her very attractive with her long flowing hair, her pretty face and that hippie kind of look that I like. I noticed that she was alone, but that could mean a lot of things and so I kept my eye on her for the next little while. I even asked David if he knew who she was and what was her story. He remembered her from some years ago but wasn't sure what her status was at the present time.

So now it's up to me to find out, but I'm scared to talk to her. I mean if I didn't take a shining to her it would be easy to strike up a conversation, but when you like someone, it's different. Week after week went by and sometimes I didn't see her, but when I did, I kept an eye on her to see if she was alone or if she knew someone I did.

Then one Sunday I saw her sitting having a coffee by herself, so I placed myself strategically in her line of sight. All of a sudden, she got up and came in my direction. My heart raced, my palms began to sweat. I told myself that if she got within ear shot of me I would say something, but what? I'll say hi and she might say hi back, and I will have broken the ice and that will be that.

As she approached the perimeter, I got ready to fire. She breeched the target area and I had to respond, it was my only hope – I had waited for this moment for so long. "Hello there, how are you," I stammered, not sure if I said that out loud or not.

"Good morning," she said. I don't remember what I said next but I seemed to feel at ease and began being myself and words just flew out of my mouth. Our conversation went back and forth with a few chuckles and without any uncomfortable silences. I found out her name was Monique and she wasn't attached. She had an older son and two daughters, none of whom lived with her. She was an artist and had a good job and had a brand new car. Monique told me she was starting over and I could tell there was pain there so I shared a little of my story with her. I remember a few tears from her and I could relate to where she was coming from.

Then we parted ways as she went into the service and I went home to ponder what just happened. Did she take a liking to me? Did my charm work? Will she actually remember me? Or maybe she is just one of those friendly ladies that will talk to anyone and make them feel special.

Tick…tick…tick. Time went slow until the next Sunday, but she wasn't there. Then I'd see her at church the odd Sunday and we would chat. Then I wouldn't see her for awhile . As time went on, we chatted on and off. Sometimes I felt like something special was actually happening, and other times, I felt like she was not on the same page.

It was winter now, and work was slow at the shop. My hours had been cut back, so I decided to hop on a plane to Florida and visit Sharon and Ken. While I was there I would use Sharon's laptop to check my emails and facebook and stuff. I got this message from my old friend, Sheryll, to contact her. So I did and I found out that she had been "running the roads" as she likes to call it – with none other than Monique.

Well I guess they met at church through someone that knew Sheryll was involved in the singles group and thought Monique might like to check it out. Anyway they started to hang out a bit, and somehow my name came up. Sheryll now told me through facebook that Monique wanted to get to know me better.

Okay, I'm in Florida. I have a week there and it usually flies by, but not this time. Time went by very slowly as I counted the minutes until I could get back home. Although, in a way it was good, because I had time to think about how I was going to connect with Monique.

Fast forward to the next Sunday at church: I was really hoping Monique would be there as I waited to see her smiling face, and there she was. Our eyes met and we ran into each other's arms and I spun her around. Just kidding! But I did ask her if I could call her later in the day and she said yes. What a relief!

I called and we set up a date for the next day. We met for a coffee at 10:00 a.m., and parted ways at 8:00 p.m. Needless to say, it went well and we decided right then and there that we would see where this would go. That was also a relief to me – because we had cut to the chase right off the bat – and I knew we had a chance.

After that, things moved slow for a week. We saw each other three times that first week, and from then until now, we've seen each other pretty much every day!

I fell deeply in love with Monique. She aroused emotions in me that had gone dormant for years. I had almost given up on ever feeling that way again, and now it was back full force. I suppose we got to know each other so quickly because of the instant connection we shared. There was a transparency and an honesty that I had never really experienced before. We shared hopes, dreams, and fears so openly, I knew something very real and very deep was taking place between the two of us.

As I came to understand Monique's journey, I discovered her deep reserves of courage and creativity. I admire her love of life and her passion for people. Unlike me, Monique isn't at all shy, so I think we make a great duo. Monique is everything I've waited for and I could not ask for more.

It wasn't long until we decided that we wanted to spend the rest of our lives together. This caused some concern from some family and friends, understandably so. But in time, all accepted our decision to marry.

We were married in the backyard of my (now our) little house on June 25, 2011 with a small group of family and friends looking on. Of course, it was David who married us, it just couldn't be any other way.

Time has moved quickly in the last year and a half of our marriage, and we continue to grow together and in Christ. We believe God brought us together and trust in Him. Our scars are healing, some of them quickly, others are taking more time. The main thing is, we are helping each other and listening to each other. I think we both have a lot of experience in doing things wrong and we have learned from that. We are not the same people we were; we have been changed, transformed if you will, by the grace of God. It's not what we have done in the past, it's what we are doing right now that matters the most.

Now I have extended family members who are very special to me, and I'm learning to love and be loved.

Chapter 17:
The Twelve Step Program and How it Saved My Life

I know that some say the Twelve Steps are the only way to get and stay sober. Others say it never worked for them, for one reason or another. A lot of people have a problem with the 'God' thing and I can understand it. Many people have been dealt a rotten hand in life! They've never had any kind of spiritual influence, or if they did, bad stuff still happened to them, stuff beyond their control. They tried praying, but things just got worse for them.

I know some people who prayed to God once... and He relieved them of their desire to drink or drug immediately, and they never had another craving. I know others that never went to church or to AA and have gotten sober, and stayed sober. So I can't honestly say there is only ONE WAY!

I will say this, though: these Twelve Steps and my higher power, Jesus Christ, worked for me! After reading my story, can you come up with any other explanation? Was it just a hundred and one coincidences or was it one big God-incidence?

Let me introduce you to the Twelve Steps as I experienced them. You'll be able to appreciate how God moved me from the depths of the abyss to the top of the mountain!

STEP ONE: We admitted that we were powerless over alcohol, and our lives were unmanageable.

Well, this was a no-brainer for me; just look at what I had done to myself! I couldn't even go across the road without a beer in my hand. My whole life revolved around alcohol, at the end. Even before that, it was pot. I had to be stoned all the time to feel normal. When I was at my worst, I used to puke every morning, I had the shakes, and my vision was blurry until I drank a beer or two... then I'd be okay!

But I still would argue to the point of fist-fighting that I wasn't an alcoholic or addict. I had become physically and mentally dependent on my drug of choice, but I lacked the smarts to put together the 'no-brainer' of my condition. It wasn't until there was, literally, nowhere else to go that I went to the Centre, and even then, I wasn't sure I had a problem!

But admitting I was powerless was the first step. At the Centre, we had been given work books with questions on each step. As we answered the questions and worked our way through the step, it began to get the feelings out. Putting things down on paper really started to help me. Actually, this book would not be possible if I hadn't written it all down. In Step One, I went back to the powerlessness and unmanage-ability of my active addiction career.

I tried to wrap my brain around this notion of powerlessness. In my trade as a mechanic, I work with a lot of equipment and machinery. If one of those machines is powerless, it simply doesn't work – it's broken and it needs repair if it's go-ing to avoid the scrap heap. That's how I began to see myself: broken, useless, and on the skids. I was definitely powerless and needed to be repaired.

I found out that addictions, for some reason, affect the surviv-al part of the brain. Imagine you are stranded without food or water, maybe for days. Eventually your brain tells your body that you need food or water. You begin to yearn for something to quench the thirst, satisfy the hunger. It's the same with drugs or alcohol. Your body begins to crave it. If there's no relief, then just like a starving person, your stomach aches, your head pounds and spins, and eventually you stop functioning. That's why withdrawals hurt so much. You're telling your body that there will be no relief. And so the cycle continues until you finally break through. You either deal with the pain, or you give in. So get this: your brain is telling your body that you need to have something mood-altering so you can be normal. So you take drugs or drink alcohol so you can feel okay. Weird, isn't it? You need to get messed up to feel normal? How does that make sense?

It doesn't. And that's how the unmanageable part of Step One came into play. I had spent the last two weeks before I got there without eating at all and sleeping just a little. In fact, all I did was drink. I was thin as a rail, a bag of bones! Everything good in my life was gone! How could I not get this step?

STEP TWO: We came to believe a power greater than ourselves could restore us to sanity.

When I first read step two, I thought sanity was a pretty strong word. But, then I got to thinking about my life, and I realized maybe I'm not far from being insane. I mean, anyone who does the things I did, and felt the way I did, had to be a little crazy, didn't they?

Look at the money I blew night after night. It was nothing to drop $1,000 a weekend, just so I could feel good and escape – that was insane!

Wherever I went, I had what I called my "paper wallet", which was the cash from work that was supposed to be deposited at the bank. But if I ran into a friend, or if someone showed up at the shop – the 'paper wallet' bankrolled our binging, lap dances, and lines of coke at four in the morning – that was insane!

I was losing my wife and my only son because I was more interested in women and parties and being wasted… and I was getting to be 40 years old… time to grow up! That was insane!

The morning I woke up and realized that here I was, 47 years old, without a bed to sleep in or anyone left to turn to, and I still got drunk on the way to the Centre – that was insane!

I really hoped this step was true. I realized "the higher power" they talked about was the God I had known as a child, but I just wasn't sure. I mean, I always knew there was a God, but would He help me after everything I had done… the hurt I had caused others, and the disappointment I was sure I had caused Him? Was He angry with me?

This step brought back all of those beautiful flannel graph stories I learned in Sunday school. You remember those colourful cut-outs they put on the green felt board? The old Bible stories I had been taught as a child flooded my mind, and I remembered how Jesus said, "Father, forgive them for they know not what they do." I recalled how He healed people and performed many miracles.

At the Centre, they used to tell us, "Don't leave five minutes before your miracle." And slowly at first, then the longer I was there, more and more I began to believe it. There really were miracles, and it seemed like I was experiencing one. I saw changes happening in me. As the fog began to lift, I started to feel better physically, mentally and spiritually. I was learning so much.

But this miracle wasn't free. There was a lot of hard work in this step about going back over life's relationships, and coming to terms with the pain of broken promises and broken possibilities. They really put you through the ringer on this step. I didn't want to have to feel all that hurt again, by reliving it. It was hard enough the first time! Like they say in the program, "Good recovery is found on the far side of despair." I was starting to see that they just might be right!

STEP THREE: We made a decision to turn our will and our lives over to the care of God (as we understood Him).

When you understand your higher power as the God I grew up with as a child, it's not that hard to do this step. Even if I didn't follow Him very well, I always believed that He was there. And the more I remembered, the more I could tell the difference between God as He is, and the God of religion and rules and regulations. The God I knew as a child was a good God; a kind, loving and gracious God. But as I grew up, He turned into an angry, stern and punishing God. I should have noticed the change, but I'm not sure I did. All I knew was there was no way I could come close to pleasing that kind of a God, so there was no point in trying. So now that I was seeing Him for who He really was, I knew I needed His help!

Did I begin Step Three at the Centre? Or did it start back in my apartment when I was being evicted? Was that when I decided I needed help? I wrote in my workbook on Step Three: "Yes, I believe I need a change. I admit I am powerless and my life is unmanageable. I have the ability to change with the help of my higher power, I'm not doing it alone. Help is available from my higher power and my peers." It was at once a powerful and humbling statement, but it felt like the breath of life.

Step Three can be so easy, but so hard at the same time. It's easy to say, okay God, You're in the driver's seat now, and I will go and do what You want me to, knowing that You are in control and will do the best for me. But it takes a lot of faith to actually believe that this will work. Sometimes life doesn't go just the way you thought it should, and you just don't understand what's going on all the time. It's like walking into the middle of a movie and things don't seem to make sense, but as you watch it from beginning to end, you see how all the parts fit together.

I still try to live by this step today. I think every Christ-follower should. But it's not so easy in practical terms. I mean, what does it look like to turn everything over to God's care? How does that affect day-to-day decision making? And how do you know the difference between His will and your will? And maybe toughest of all, how does that stop me from drinking? Well, I haven't seen any lightning bolts yet, but what I have done is learned how to pray, and try to listen. I read the Bible and use my gut, and it almost always takes me in the right direction. And when it doesn't, I try to learn from it, to see how and why it ended up the way it did. If I think about how it all took place, I will eventually see where I took the control from God and as Frank Sinatra (or Ol' Blue Eyes) put it, "I did it my way."

In the trial-and-error journey of Step Three, here's what I learned (straight from my journal):

I am worth the effort, I am one of God's creations, and I am a good person. When I first came here, I had a really hard time making decisions and taking action. But now I've been faced with some serious decisions, and with a little time and thought, I get it figured out for the best. I believe I've been keeping my priorities pretty straight.

One day, I wrote this letter to God:

Dear God,
Hi. This is a letter from Billy, one of Your creations. I'm very thankful for the chance You have given to me to get to know You better since I've been at the Centre. I always believed You were there, but bringing me here shows me that You have a purpose in life for me. I've decided to let Your will be done in my life. I'm just going to trust in You.

STEPS FOUR & FIVE

FOUR: We made a searching and fearless moral inventory of ourselves.
FIVE: We admitted to God, to ourselves and to another human being the exact nature of our wrongs.

These two steps are by far the most painful, yet they can also be very rewarding, if done properly. They ask you to evaluate, and as best you can, correct issues that involve resentment, faults, fears, sexual conduct, and harm done to others, and yourself.

I found out that resentments are the number one offender. We were told to write down the people we resented and why. What part of our lives had those people affected or harmed?

We were to include individuals, institutions or principles that we were angry at.

First on my list was my sister, Sharon! She was the reason I was here! She pulled the rug out from under my feet when I wasn't looking! My list continued with other people, places, and things I was angry at. It says in the Big Book that when we "harbor" such feelings, we shut ourselves off from the sunlight of the spirit.

Then, we were told to write the causes and effects of these resentments, and all the wrongs that we had done. Remember, we had to be completely honest about this or it wouldn't work. The lists continued on with the wrongs others have done to us; anger, fear and shame were next. Then came the dreaded subject of sex!

My lists became longer and longer as I worked through Step Four. I wrote everything I could think of – good, bad and ugly – it didn't matter to me. I was there to get better and if they said being honest was the only way, that's the way I did it… dump it all!

By the time I'd completed the catalogue of Step Four, I was in my last few days at the Centre. I had worked hard every day to get this far. A few of my peers and I were selected to do Step Five before we were to leave. I thought at the time that it was good enough to complete Step Four before I left, admitting all these things to myself, opening my eyes to my part in my demise. My counsellor, Ralph, told me that to try to avoid this humbling experience and keep certain facts to myself could leave me very vulnerable to drink again, and that I needed to do a thorough housecleaning. It was necessary to tell someone else my story and be entirely honest if I expected to live a long and happy life of sobriety.

Reluctantly, I agreed. A quick survey of the change in me in the last 28 days told me I had nothing to fear. I had trusted the process so far, and it had worked. This was just one more step of trust and obedience, so I did it. I went to a room, and a man whom I'd never seen before was sitting there waiting. He had been hand-picked by the Centre to listen to people tell their story in Step Five. He didn't speak much, only to ask a few questions here and there. I was in there for about an hour and a half, but it only seemed like a few minutes – it was weird! Then it was over. I'd done it!

I left the room feeling uplifted – really close to God, actually. I went for a walk alone with my thoughts, and my Big Book. I read through the first Five Steps, like it tells you to do at this point. Searching deeply through each one of them, I had to make sure I had done them to the best of my ability, leaving nothing out. It had to be a strong foundation.

Later, after I left the Centre, Natalie helped me a lot with these two steps. Although I had written and said many things in Steps Four and Five, some of them were still kind of spinning around in my head. In our time together, I was able to really deal with issues and let go of them or continue to work on them as need be. I was also able to go even deeper into my Fifth Step with her as I remembered things about my past. I'm pretty sure that I wouldn't have made it through that first year without her help and guidance.

STEPS SIX & SEVEN

SIX: We were entirely ready to have God remove all of our character defects.
SEVEN: We humbly asked Him to remove all of our shortcomings.

The key to mastering these two steps is serious reflection. You've got to get alone and open your heart and soul to God. So, after my Fifth Step, I went out into the forest. It was spring… and you can picture it… the trees were budding, the air was full of life, and I was sitting on a rock taking in all of God's great wonders and reading my Big Book. I was ready to let God remove all the things that I admitted were wrong. Will He actually take them right now, every one? What if I don't do it perfectly? If I still cling to something, will He help me let it go? I asked God to help me.

I read directly from the Big Book, "My Creator God, I am now willing that You should have all of me, good and bad. I pray that You remove from me every single defect of character which stands in the way of my usefulness to You, and my fellows. Grant me strength as I go from here, to do Your bidding."

I got up and began walking down a narrow path. Tears began to come to my eyes, and I wept openly, wondering what was going to happen to me. I was to leave the Centre the next day, and I didn't have a dime to my name, a job, a place to live – nothing! As I slowly walked the path, a leafy canopy formed overhead. The trees towered thirty feet tall on each side and formed two forest walls along the path. With all this beautiful nature around me, I was talking to God the best way I knew how at the time. I can't explain in words how genuinely supernatural this was, but I'll try. I know I've already talked about this, but I'm saying it again. It's important!

As I turned a corner and followed the trail along, I became almost blinded by this bright light. It was the sun, beaming down, right exactly over top of me. I mean exactly! There was only a few feet on each side of the trail where the tall trees had left a gap, and the sun was right there! There was shade all around me on each side, but the sun shone down on me like a spot light! Bright rays illuminated this very spot, perhaps only a few minutes each day, and I had stumbled on it at just the right moment. I had never prayed a prayer so earnestly before, and now, just as I was wondering whether God would answer, here I was basking in His glory!

I stopped dead in my tracks and looked up into the brightest sunbeam I've ever seen. I didn't actually hear God, but I felt Him say, "Everything is going to be okay. Don't worry, just trust in Me." A strange calm came over me, something I had never experienced before, and right then and there, I knew it would be okay. I didn't know how, I just knew it would! I walked out of the forest that day a new person!

If you think that is weird, listen to this: ten years later, almost to the day, I went back to the Centre. I decided to take a stroll down memory lane and see if I could find that spot. Well, it was a cloudy, rainy day as I trudged through the muddy trails, trying to remember exactly where this vivid experience had happened to me. After some time, I navigated through the maze of trails and found it. At that moment, the sun broke through the clouds and shone down on me. It was only out for about ten seconds that entire day, but it came out when I was in that spot. Was this just another coincidence or was it a God-incident?

174

STEPS EIGHT & NINE

EIGHT: We made a list of all persons we had harmed, and we became willing to make amends to them all.
NINE: We made direct amends to such people wherever possible, except when to do so would harm them or others.

When I pulled into Sudbury, I stayed in a motel, owned by a guy I had ploughed for. My sister, Ardie, had given me a bit of cash, and Joe cut me a deal for a week's stay. It wasn't anything special, but there was a bed and a roof… and a crummy little TV. First thing on my agenda was to get hooked up with Natalie, who had been out of the Centre for two weeks by the time I got out. Our reunion took place over coffee after an AA meeting.

Now that I was back home, I began to work through Step Eight. If you've ever seen the show My Name is Earl, you've got some kind of idea what that's like. I wish it was as funny in real life, but the truth is, it's painful, and it doesn't always work out. You'd love it if everybody forgave you and gave you a hug; if they were happy for you and your new-found life, but it's not always that way.

I had a lot of people to make amends to. Some were really receptive, and relationships were genuinely healed. Some just shrugged it off and said, "Hey, no sweat." But there were those who just couldn't handle it. They were bitter, unkind and demanding. Funny thing is, that some of the most forgiving were people I really burned, and some of the meanest were people that were way down my list! Go figure.

One time, I went back to Sudbury after five years of sobriety, and a guy named Gerry accosted me because I had owed him some money for coke. It was from along time ago and had forgotten. "Hey buddy, where's my money?" he demanded.

He was obviously wasted, and to be honest, I couldn't remember the details. After all, that was years ago, and happened in a distant galaxy... but he reminded me of the deal we had made, so I asked him, "Well Gerry, how much do I owe you?"

He just lost it in a rant, "Man after everything we've been through, I never thought you'd stiff me like that!" He went on and on. "So like what are you going to do about it, eh?"

I thought he was going to punch me in the head. So I told him, "Listen, I don't have any money right now (and that was true, I really didn't!), but next time I come up, I'll bring you some."

I could tell he wasn't buying it, so I got away as quick as I could. At that moment, I realized there was another item on my list... people I owe drug money to. Heavy sigh.

The next time I went up to Sudbury, I brought some extra cash. I looked all over for Gerry, but couldn't find him. So I gave the money to another guy I owed dope money to. Every time I go back there, I keep my eye open for Gerry, and I know what I'll do. I'll take him straight to a bank machine, and give him the money I owe him.

Making amends isn't just about saying you're sorry. Sometimes it costs you money you don't have! More than that, there's a fine line between Step Eight and Step Nine. It takes some serious wisdom, and a lot of honesty with yourself to know who to talk to, and who to let go. You have to be very careful you don't do more damage than you have already done.

So I wrote a long list, and over some time, was able to talk to most of the people that I felt I needed to. Again, Natalie was very instrumental in this step for me. Beside the relationships where I might do more harm than good, there were some people I just had to stay away from until I was stronger, but I got around to them eventually. And like Gerry, there are situations I've just plain forgotten, and a few that are still pending. But like Earl, I plan to keep making amends as long as there are amends to be made.

Along the way, I got some negative reactions about having 'gone religious.' The truth is, at this point I still hadn't fully crossed the line. Something very real and spiritual had begun in my life, and I was making my way back to where I belonged, but I definitely wasn't a full on Christ-follower just yet. Natalie, the woman I was with, was still married and I wasn't divorced either. And while she was a great help to me along the way, our relationship didn't really honour God, and to be frank, it had its own dysfunctions.

STEPS TEN, ELEVEN & TWELVE

TEN: We continued to take a personal inventory and when we were wrong, we would promptly admit it.
ELEVEN: We sought through prayer and meditation to improve our conscious contact with God as we understood Him, praying only for knowledge of His will for us and the power to carry it out.
TWELVE: Having had a spiritual awakening as a result of these steps, we try to carry this message to alcoholics and to practice these principles in all our affairs.

I try to live out these three steps continuously in my life as I grow in my recovery. It's been over ten years now, and it's still a work in progress. But admitting you're wrong can be difficult, and it seems it's not something we're taught. Everyone wants to be right, don't they? We argue about who's right and wrong all the time!

Well, Step Ten tells us different. Take personal inventory and when we're wrong, admit it. Say what? Admit we are wrong? I can tell you that this step took a little getting used to. Just to admit, "Yeah, you're right, and I'm wrong," seems so easy to say, but actually, it's not at first. You have to practice it – and let me tell you – I did over and over again. What I've learned is that you have to constantly be open to the fact of your short-sightedness; it's a matter of continual self-critique. And you have to be open to others in a new way that isn't always comfortable. You've got to avoid those knee-jerk judgments and learn to listen instead.

Today, I have no problem admitting I'm wrong. I don't have to be right all the time. And guess what? It takes a real load off, you know! On the other hand, if a situation comes up that I am right about, I don't have to gloat about it either, and say, "I told you so!" I can just go about my business and not have to look or feel better than anyone. Because the truth is, I've been wrong more than my fair share.

Prayer has become a huge part of my life, as Step Eleven recommends. Looking back, although I didn't know it at the time, the knowledge of God's will that I prayed for brought me here, to Cambridge. Each little fork in the road on my path, needed to be chosen... first by God, then by me. I needed to make a choice with my free will each and every time, but I wanted it to be God's will, too.

There were times I knew exactly what God's will was, and others, I wasn't so sure. The process of learning to trust that the thoughts regarding the decision I was about to make were from God was a tough one. A statement from the Twelve Steps and Twelve Traditions has stuck with me over the years: I know that "of myself I am nothing, the Father doeth the works." Years later, I discovered it was based on a Bible verse (John 14:10). Sometimes you just have to trust that God guides you when you put your life in His hands.

I began the spiritual awakening that Step Twelve talks about, way back at the Centre in the spring of 1999. In the forest that day, I had an experience I will never forget, nor can I ever deny. But it was just a start. I still hadn't surrendered my life to Jesus. That came when I finally returned to the church of my youth and asked Jesus to be my Lord and Saviour. But there's no question something miraculous happened to me in that forest glade, and I was never the same after.

I know that doesn't fit the standard picture of how salvation comes to people, but that's how it happened to me. From that point on, I knew that I was headed in the right direction. No drug or drink had ever pointed me in that direction. The way I was living and the thoughts in my head at the time never took me in the right direction, but my higher power did.

God reached out His hand that warm spring day, and started to lead me out of the darkness. It didn't happen overnight. It took years of work and a million prayers to get me out of where I had gotten myself to: lost so deep. And because of that gift of life, I developed a deep desire to help others find the way. I began to get involved in reaching out to people who were like I was wherever I found them. And they were everywhere! Through groups like ROOF and AA, or my workplace, or through church, I just seemed to discover people who were somewhere I used to be. Sometimes God has let me get involved in a true recovery story and sometimes I've watched sadly as they were consumed by their addiction. I prefer the former.

Today I'm a different person! People that haven't seen me for years can tell I am different right away, and I'm not talking physical appearance. When you see a small child and then you don't see them for years, they have changed so much. That's how good recovery works: if you look in the mirror every day, you don't see yourself changing – it happens so slowly – but it happens, and it's noticeable to others.

I have become involved in the church, and don't attend AA all that much anymore. I find what I need from God and have a strong support group in the church. I will never forget what AA has done for me, how AA saved my life and brought me back to God, and I cherish it.

I try my best to live by all these steps. I sometimes have to go back to one and work on it a bit, as life throws the odd curve ball. And I'm no spiritual giant, either. I can honestly say that I haven't read the whole Bible but I'm working on it. I'm not the best reader, and it's not the easiest book to read. But I still get good direction from God through His Word and prayer, and with a little help from my friends.

I'm a perfect example of answered prayer. My Mom and Dad prayed for me for years and never lived to see their prayers answered – and that, I truly regret. Their friends prayed for me for years, and when I see them on Manitoulin Island or back in Sudbury, I know my life-change gives them hope, just like their prayers remind me that I was never alone, even at the worst moments.

I've always heard that God doesn't wear a watch; He does things in His time. Don't ever give up, keep on praying. God is at work, even when you can't see it or feel it, or even believe He's there. That's why I wrote this book. I wanted people to know what God has done for me. But I also wanted to encourage you to never, ever stop believing. There is a Hope. His name is Jesus.

Billy Moore

An Afterword about Angels

I've been eager to put this section somewhere in my book...
but I just couldn't find the right place. I was about to leave
things the way they were, but that didn't seem right either. So
here it is... a little doff of the hat to some wonderful people
who made the difference in my life. I call them 'angels' and
here's a little poem I found written by Christine Bruness that
pretty much sums up why:

For Angels Everywhere

Appear in all shapes and sizes
Non-judgmental; nice; non-invasive
Graceful; good-hearted; God's messengers & helpers
Empathic; extremely compassionate; ethereal
Lovely; loving; lifesavers; labour to promote peace, healing,
positivity, wellness & goodness
Serene; soft; sweet caregivers; selfless; sacred protectors

I've always heard that angels can come in strange packages,
and I think I've run into some of the strangest in my journeys.
Now, I know the Bible talks about angels as supernatural
servants of God. I've read about Gabriel and Michael, the
cherubim and the seraphim, and I believe in them. But when
I talk about angels here, I'm talking about some of the people
God sends across your path to pick you up when you're
down for the count, or to set you back on the right track when
you've strayed, or to remind you where you were going when
you seem to have forgotten. Like lamp posts along a dark
road, there always seems to be another when the light from
the last one has grown dim.

My first encounter with an angel!

These angels show up when you least expect it… and maybe when you least deserve it, too! That's how it was one night in 1994. Coming back from a race one night, my buddy, Al and I were heavily intoxicated. We had just gotten into Sudbury. Somehow, the ratchet device that holds the race truck on the trailer was not properly engaged and let go. The race truck had a broken drive shaft, so there was nothing to stop the wheels from turning. As we were rounding the corner from Van Horne Hill to Paris Street, it just rolled off the trailer. It bounced across the median with cars coming right at it as we watched helplessly. It rolled down the street, just in front of the cop shop, believe it or not! It picked up momentum as it crossed lanes of traffic, cars dodging it, the truck probably hit at least 30 kilometres an hour. A stranger came out of nowhere on the street, ran beside it and steered it to safety. I pulled a U-turn – right in front of the police station with my truck and empty trailer – and sped over to retrieve the race truck. After stopping, I went to find this guy. He didn't say much. He was old with ragged clothes and a scruffy beard – he looked like a bum. I turned around for a second to do something, and when I turned back, he was gone! He disappeared just as mysteriously as he had shown up! Was he a guardian angel? Okay… maybe that's a little over the top. But we were drunk as skunks, and somehow managed to get the powerless race truck back on the trailer before the cops got there. I don't really understand what the whole story was about… but to this day, it feels like there was some kind of an angel involved.

Denise

I mentioned Denise earlier; she was the girl who went with me to the Centre that first time. She fits into the angel category, too. She was a biker chick – tough looking, tattoos here and there, and a rough life, too. She'd been through it with an abusive husband. I met her at the Nic… the Nickel City Bar in Sudbury. I was right at the end of my rope and I needed a woman in my life at the time – any woman! And as any addict will tell you, a bad relationship is better than no relationship.

So Denise was looking pretty good to me that night. Of course, her ex-husband was on the scene, too. That should have been a flag. According to Denise, he was beating her all the time. Truth is, she might have been beating him. But somehow, she became an angel in my life. Denise knew about AA, and actually gave me my first Big Book (Alcoholics Anonymous). She was on for the ride that life changing night that I began my journey.

That fateful day, April 13, 1999, Denise and I had a few beers as we left Sudbury around noon. Needing a little more liquid courage as we got closer to Elliot Lake, we stopped in Spanish, Ontario, my dad's hometown. How ironic is that? It seemed like a good place to grab a few more drinks. So we stayed there a few hours, played pool, and eventually as the evening came on, I drank what proved to be my last beer. I drank it, without being aware that I would never drink again. I'm not sure if I would have enjoyed it more, or less, if I had known!

As we climbed into the truck, neither of us knew what a significant encounter I was about to have on entering the Centre, or how dramatic the change would be. When I look back, I'm grateful for Denise's presence, and sad, too, because I don't think she ever got free herself.

Natalie

And of course, I'll always remember Natalie as an angel in my life. She talked and talked to me about the importance of family, and helped me to make amends with my sister, plus to contact my son. I have much to thank her for! She loved me when I didn't have a dime to my name, and I wasn't used to that. She was attending school and I was driving taxi odd hours, but we did make time to spend together. Sometimes, I just slept while she studied!

Now, I realize that I was totally dependent on her and this was wrong! I was fairly early in recovery. For the first time, I had to face things without masking them with drugs or alcohol. My feelings were very sensitive, and she helped me look at things logically; that calmed my nerves and helped me get through things without worrying too much. She was like my "sponsor" from AA. Because she had a lot of knowledge about AA stuff, I relied on her. I could tell her anything and everything without her judging me. It was like I did my Step Five over and over again with her. She was a BIG part of my support system – very necessary when you leave Rehab, but you are not supposed to fall in love with the person you confide in and they are supposed to be of the same sex.

I felt that I was staying under her 'wings' – angel wings! I felt safe from the outside world. I knew that I wasn't strong enough yet to face everything out there. It wasn't meant to be, but I thank God for the time we had together.

Mike and Jamie

One of the toughest parts of recovery is figuring out what to
do with your spare time... you know, the time you spent doing the things that ruined your life (which is why you needed
recovery in the first place). It can be a pretty lonely walk,
unless you find some people who understand where you've
been. But God sent me a couple of angels when I first got back
to Sudbury – Jamie and Mike – two great guys from Southern
Ontario who had been into some hardcore programs at the
Sally Ann in Sudbury.

They were both about ten years younger than me, but we
seemed to hit it off from the get-go. I met up with them at
my Aftercare program at Pinehurst. We started hanging out
together in our spare time. That was a good thing, because
I had a lot of it in those days since I wasn't working. Idle
hands, my mother used to say, are the devil's workshop. I
joined their AA home group and went to meetings all over
the city with them on other nights of the week. We would go
out to movies or just hang out at their house and talk. Jamie
joined my ball team and played with us for one year. Jamie
was the guy who became God's catalyst in getting me back on
the faith path. He took me to the Salvation Army church in
Sudbury, and that started my wheels turning in the direction
I should go.

Hailey

As soon as I moved to Cambridge, I knew I had to find
some help. It was a pretty rough transition moving from
the hometown to a place where, contrary to the old Cheers
theme, nobody knows your name! To make matters worse, I
had gone from the top of the heap to the bottom, financially,

relationally, and occupationally. My first job at the muffler and brake shop was as low as I could go in the garage business. I was the rookie go-fer with thirty years' experience... and truth be told, in my state of mind, I couldn't handle much else. My confidence was gone, at least, what little I had, but I did have the determination to get out of the mess I had made of my life. All I needed was a little help.

So God sent another angel. Her name was Hailey. I got in touch with an addiction counselling facility in Kitchener, and Hailey was the incredibly gifted counsellor they connected me with. She was definitely heaven-sent, and for about three years she guided my path and kept me out of relapse trouble. I felt comfortable with her right from the start, and we began an even deeper process of digging up the junk in my life. We revisited my Fifth Step together, and because she had come to truly know me, she could help me reassess the meaning of my actions. Hailey saw a lot of strength in me that I didn't have a clue I possessed. She helped me recognize that there was still some goodness within, and that I needed to forgive myself and love myself. I know it sounds a little cliché, but when you've let down as many people in your life as I have, that's not an easy job... it takes months of reprogramming. One of the most powerful tools she gave me was a piece by Virginia Satir called I Am Me, I Am Okay. It helped me to gain a healthier perspective on life.

Eventually, our time together came to an end; all healthy counselling does. I had formed such a deep bond with Hailey. I remember telling her that I might be like the Bill Murray character in the movies What About Bob, showing up everywhere she went. Thankfully with the 'baby steps' I learned from her, that didn't happen. I did see Hailey a couple of times after that. She requested that I do a TV commercial to promote the addiction counselling facility and I gladly did it in return for all the help they had given me. Hailey moved onto another city and I lost touch with her, but I will never forget how much she helped me in my recovery.

Sandy

Another one of those divinely appointed angels was a lady named Sandy. Sandy is one of those individuals who just seems to care about people wherever she finds them, and she seems to run into them all over the place. She ran into me at a suicide prevention course that ROOF had sent me on. The course was being offered at a church I had noticed as I drove up and down highway 24 in Cambridge. The church was Calvary Assembly. My sister had told me that David Courey, who had pastored my Dad in Sudbury, was now here in Cambridge at Calvary. At this point, though, I hadn't even thought about going there. In fact, I was a little leery about going to this course, because it was happening in a Pentecostal church. Knowing that David was there wasn't an encouragement, either. I could remember those awkward drives I used to give him when we would fix his car back in the Sudbury days. He'd just sit there and strike up a conversation… and I'd feel like God was peering into my life… ugh!

But since I was facing old ghosts anyway, and this course was part of what I had to do, I just ratcheted up my determination and went. And who did I meet but Sandy! She was such an easy, non-judgmental person to talk to. With my defenses down, I just got kind of lulled into a spiritual conversation with her. Of course, I didn't know that at the time… I just found myself telling her things I wouldn't normally tell a perfect stranger!

As we kept talking, next thing I knew we were talking about Sudbury. It just so happened that Sandy had recently been in Sudbury for a conference, and was billeted through a church called (of all things!) Glad Tidings. She had stayed with an elderly woman who was remarkably friendly and talkative. It also just so happened that lady had been one of my Mom's best friends when I was growing up, Mrs. Nelder. Well, we reminisced about Mrs. Nelder and Glad Tidings, and somehow all that talking awoke some warm memories about the good old days. It lasted only a short while before my knee-jerk revulsion at everything Pentecostal returned. But it was the foot in the door. Now whenever I passed by that church, my thoughts were no longer just negative. I began to recall some genuine Jesus moments from the past.

I wasn't near ready to take the step of returning to church even after Sandy invited me, but her kindness left an impression; her words were like a constant dripping that eventually wears through the stone of a closed heart. It was a couple of months later that I finally did decide to go to Calvary. It was the Sunday between Christmas and New Year's, and I was lost. I had nobody to just be with, to hang out with, to belong to, it seemed. I walked into the place sure of my anonymity. Who could possibly know me here? It was a big church, and while I didn't expect to talk to anyone, I was kind of hoping I'd see Sandy again. And sure enough, there she was sitting up near the front. We connected after the service, and besides her warm welcome, she re-introduced me to David. It was the connection I needed to get me over the hump. So I thank her for being one of the lamp posts along the way, and if it wasn't for her, who knows if I ever would have made it through the doors of that church.

Sheryll

Definitely a character… that's what Sheryll is! I met her one Sunday after church over at David's house. Sheryll was fun and outgoing. She had a crack and a comment about everything, and she made you laugh out loud. As we got to know each other, I discovered that we had something in common besides David and Eileen: she had also lived in Sudbury, though she travelled with a different crowd than I did. So we hung out a bit from time to time and even tried dating for a short while. It didn't take too long to see that wouldn't work. We both agreed that we weren't compatible, but we have remained friends and still connect every once in awhile.

Sheryll was the one who nominated me for the Courage to Comeback Award. She really felt in her heart that I was a deserving nominee. She had heard my story, and gotten to know the 'new' me, and the two just didn't compute. She wrote a really nice nomination letter about me and sent it in to CAMH. She told me what she was doing and I thanked her, but forgot all about it until one day, I got the call that I had been selected as a recipient. I was thrilled… until I realized I'd have to go on stage and make a speech before 1,500 people! Then I wasn't so excited anymore. I wanted to strangle her.

Sheryll was also instrumental in making the connection between my wife Monique and I. Of course Sheryll is a real social butterfly and is actively involved in a Christian Single's Group. She had invited Monique to a singles' event, and on the way home my name came up. After a bit of chatting on the subject of me, Monique seemed interested. Then Sheryll became matchmaker and the rest is history.

Ed

Although Ed hasn't played a large role in my life, God used him to let me know He was watching over me. When I first showed up in Cambridge, I didn't know a soul except for my niece, Tracey. I had gone to some AA meetings, but really hadn't made a friend. When it came to looking for work, here I was, a 47-year-old licensed mechanic whose brain wasn't near ready to work on a car. After sending over twenty resumes out for all kinds of positions (delivery jobs, day labourer, and construction worker), Ed was the first guy to respond. When he heard my story, he gave me my first job down here. A month or so later, Ed rented me my first place. He also let me store my race trucks for free in his company lot. Ed was a simple, Christian guy who knew I needed a break.

Ed now brings his vehicles to the shop I work at for repairs, and we get to chat like we did every month when he came to collect the rent. He always talks about how good God is, and I guess that's not hard to see, since his business is thriving and he is probably a multi-millionaire. Don't get me wrong, he has worked hard to get where he is and he has always put God first and God has blessed him in many ways. Ed helped us financially with the soap box derby, and got a framed collage of pictures to proudly hang on his wall as a thank you to commemorate the day. Ed is involved heavily in his church and helps people like me regularly for the glory of God.

Anita

Anita started working for the shop I work at, doing the books once a week. She was a breath of fresh air when she first came into the place. With her bubbly, friendly personality, and her gift of the gab, she was the kind of person you wanted to be around; someone you'd like to get to know. I noticed something different about her right away, but I couldn't put my finger on it. She got to know everybody in the shop pretty quickly. It wasn't long before I found out that she is a Christian and that she attends the church that Calvary planted in Hespeler a few years ago, so we know some of the same people.

Anita isn't just a good talker, she's a great listener, too. If she catches me when I'm feeling down, she'll ask what's going on, and somehow she seems to know just what to ask, because I find myself giving her pretty honest answers. I don't think she has the slightest clue how her insights and counsel have encouraged me. I've become good friends with her and her husband, Albert, and her two girls Kara and Elana and I hang out with all of them from time to time. In fact, Elana was the soap box derby champion a few years ago. It is always nice to see Anita's happy face and have a little chat with her on the day that she comes into the shop. Anita is just another lamp post on the way that reminds me I'm heading in the right direction.

Today

These last thirteen years have been a completely new life for me. In many ways, emerging from the shadows of drugs and alcohol has not only meant transition from darkness to light (like it did in the woods at the Centre that afternoon in 1999), it has also been a coming of age. It wasn't until I was 47 that I was ready to leave the rebellious teen years behind and begin to grow up.

I had been arrested at age 17, which means that for thirty years, my growth, development, and maturity had been stymied between 17 and 47. I spent three decades locked up behind the bars of drugs and alcohol. It wasn't until the series of events that began to unfold at the Centre that I could actually imagine freedom from bondage to the person I had become. But in that split second in the sun, on the forest path amid those tall pines, I began to walk into hope.

From that day to this one, I have continued on that path, finding hope at almost every corner. I'd be a liar to make it sound like each day is brighter than the last, and that dark times are a thing of the past. Substance abuse allowed me to escape reality, and slip into the matrix where everything is beautiful, even if unreal. The flipside truth is that in the drug-free world where everything is real, it's not always beautiful. But as the apostle Paul said, "By the grace of God, I am what I am" (1 Corinthians 15: 10). And that grace has seen me through some pretty tough times.

Grace has also led me into some truly wonderful moments. I've met some amazing angels and some faithful friends along the way. I've been places and shared my story with people I could never have imagined. And now I'm sharing it with you. Pretty amazing, isn't it, for a guy who had lost everything, and couldn't see his way into the next disaster.

If you're travelling somewhere and you go in the wrong direction long enough, you know you're going the wrong way. If you go the wrong way long enough, you may even get lost. Well that's what drugs and alcohol did to me. They took me in the wrong direction for a long time, and I got so lost! But the miracle is that God walks paths you'd never expect to find Him on, and when you're lost, He isn't. I'm so glad He found me, forgave me, and infused me with hope.

I owe it all to Jesus Christ, and all those people who prayed for me for all those lost years. I am not yet what I should be, but, thank God, I'm not what I once was! I'm standing straight and tall... and I keep walking into hope each new day.

Ardith's Remarks:

I'm so proud to see the man my little brother has become. Bill has been drug and alcohol free for thirteen years. He has been involved with the youth in many ways by Racing Against Drugs, building demolition derby cars for the pastor, and soap box derby cars for the younger kids annual soap box derby at the church. He has made progress in reconnecting with his son, Tyler. I am proud of my little brother.

Sharon's Remarks:

Writing this piece has been a labour of love. I have used Bill's words almost exclusively. These have been taken from his many journals, notes and personal conversations. We are all thrilled with what God has done in Bill's life and are encouraged to believe for those who have not yet found their way.

*Billy 1956; Billy & Dad 1972; Billy, Dad & Tyler 1977; Billy & Mom 1973;
Billy's Super Bee*

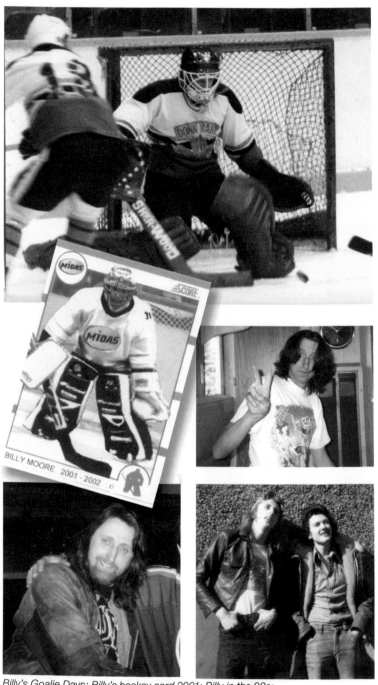

*Billy's Goalie Days; Billy's hockey card 2001; Billy in the 90s;
Billy & buddy in the 90s; Billy & Dave in the 70s*

Racing Against Drugs Mud Truck 2003; Mud Truck in newspaper article;
Billy & UFO 454; Billy's van

Going racing with my pit crew; Tough Truck jumping, Racing Against Drugs tailgate 2003; Tuff Truck Racing Against Drugs; Billy & Pastor of Disastor car crew; Calvary crew & Pastor of Disastor; Billy & Car 31 crew

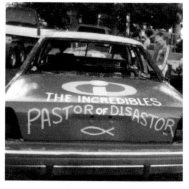

Pastor of Disastor Car 31 rear; Smashed up derby car;
Smashed up Pastor of Disastor; Pastor of Disastor (David Courey) & Billy

Courage to Come Back Award Recipient – Cambridge Times *news article;
Receiving the award, with Sharon, Billy, Tyler & Ardith; Ninth Annual Soap Box
Derby 2012; Billy & Soap Box Derby starting gate; Soap Box Derby Finish!*

Ken & Billy; Ardith & John; Sharon, Billy & Ardith; Ernie;
Billy with the TTC Creative boys – Jim, Dave (Coop) & Brian

Billy & Monique's Wedding Day; Just Married; Billy's 1987 Suburban (Badburban)